Gambling A

The Easy Guide to Stop Gambling, ~~~~~
What's Behind Your Addiction and Learn How to
Terminate It Now

By: Rick Conall

© Copyright 2020 by Rick Conall- All rights reserved.

This document is geared towards providing exact and reliable information in regards to the topic and issue covered. The publication is sold with the idea that the publisher is not required to render accounting, officially permitted, or otherwise, qualified services. If advice is necessary, legal or professional, a practiced individual in the profession should be ordered.

- From a Declaration of Principles which was accepted and approved equally by a Committee of the American Bar Association and a Committee of Publishers and Associations.

In no way is it legal to reproduce, duplicate, or transmit any part of this document in either electronic means or in printed format. Recording of this publication is strictly prohibited and any storage of this document is not allowed unless with written permission from the publisher. All rights reserved.

The information provided herein is stated to be truthful and consistent, in that any liability, in terms of inattention or otherwise, by any usage or abuse of any policies, processes, or directions contained within is the solitary and utter responsibility of the recipient reader. Under no circumstances will any legal responsibility or blame be held against the publisher for any reparation, damages, or monetary loss due to the information herein, either directly or indirectly.

Respective authors own all copyrights not held by the publisher.

The information herein is offered for informational purposes solely and is universal as so. The presentation of the information is without a contract or any type of guarantee assurance.

The trademarks that are used are without any consent, and the publication of the trademark is without permission or backing by the trademark owner. All trademarks and brands within this book are for clarifying purposes only and are owned by the owners themselves, not affiliated with this document.

TABLE OF CONTENTS

CHAPTER 1: AN INTRODUCTION TO GAMBLING ... 6

CHAPTER 2: GAMBLING AND ITS HISTORY 13

2.1 What actually is gambling? 13
2.2 A Brief History of Gambling 20
2.3 Types of Gambling 37

CHAPTER 3: GAMBLING: MYTHS. PSYCHOLOGY AND FACTS 45

CHAPTER 4: PROBLEM AND COMPULSIVE GAMBLING: SIGNS, SYMPTOMS, AND CAUSES ... 99

4.1 Pathological gambling 104
4.2 Gambling Addiction Signs and Symptoms 108
4.3 Causes and Risk Factors for Gambling Addiction 110
4.4 Triggers 116
4.5 Gambling Addiction Facts and Effects 123

CHAPTER 5: EFFECTS ON FAMILY AND RELATIONSHIPS 128

5.1 Effects of Problem Gambling on Families 128
5.2 Impacts on Family Environments 130
5.3 Effects on the Health and Wellbeing of Family Members 134

CHAPTER 6: HOW CAN FAMILY RESCUE PROBLEM GAMBLER AND CONTROL FINANCES 139

6.1 Tips for Family Members 143

6.2 Looking After your Finances 151

6.3 Speak with a financial advisor 154

CHAPTER 7: BEATING GAMBLING ADDICTION THROUGH SELF-MANAGEMENT 157

7.1 Therapy 162

7.2 Self-help groups 162

7.3 Successful Problem Treatment 166

7.4 Gambling Addiction Treatment Center 168

CONCLUSION 173

REFERENCES 175

CHAPTER 1: An Introduction to Gambling

Gambling has been defined in a number of ways. The definitions we find in dictionaries and other scholarly articles do vary in their selection of words. Still, contextually, they converge on one single-most critical fact, that is, gambling entails betting or staking or risking or jeopardizing or endangering something of value in anticipation of future monetary (or any other tangible) outcome contingent upon mere chance or accident. In short, gambling can be best described as putting your precious things in danger in the hope of uncertain future benefits. This process can be preceded by calculations or by taking the lead from past results, but they do not lend authenticity to the process and its outcome. Thus, gambling's heinous and perilous pervasiveness in today's world has become irrational and questionable both from the point of gamblers and the people advocating and patronizing this activity.

The results of gambling games can be decided by chance alone, either through the random activity of a tossed pair of dice or ball on a roulette wheel, or through physical ability, preparation, or prowess in athletic competitions, or a combination of strategy and chance. The rules that govern gambling games often misrepresent the relationship between the game's components, which depends on ability and chance, so that some players can manipulate the game to serve their own interests. Knowledge of the game is, therefore, useful to play poker or bet on horse racing but is of very little use to purchase lottery tickets or play slot machines.

A gambler may engage in the game itself while gambling on its outcome (card games, craps), or he may be prevented from participating actively in an activity in which he has personal stakes (professional sports, lottery). Without the accompanying betting activity, some games are dull or almost meaningless and are rarely played unless wagering takes place (coin tossing, poker, dice games, lotteries). In other sports, gambling is not necessarily part of the game, and the correlation is merely traditional and not necessary for the performance of the match itself (horse racing, soccer pools). Casinos and racetracks, which are commercial establishments, may arrange to gamble when it is easy to acquire a portion of the money wagered by patrons by participating as a favorite party in the game, renting space, or withdrawing a portion of the betting pool. Some very large-scale activities (horse racing, lotteries) usually require business and professional organizations to present and maintain them effectively.

A rough estimate of the approximate amount of money lawfully wagered in the world every year is around $10 trillion (illegal gambling may even surpass that figure). Lotteries are the world's leading form of gambling in terms of total turnover. State-licensed or state-operated lotteries expanded rapidly during the late 20th century in Europe and the United States and are widely distributed worldwide. Organized soccer pools can be found in almost all European countries, most countries in South America, Australia, and a few countries in Africa and Asia. Most of these countries also provide wagering on other sporting events, whether state-organized or state-licensed.

In English-speaking countries and France, betting on horse racing is a leading form of gambling. It exists in many other countries too. Wherever horse racing is famous, it has typically become a major business with its newspapers and other publications, comprehensive statistical services, self-styled experts offering betting advice, and sophisticated communication networks providing information to betting centers, bookmakers, and their employees, and employees involved in horse care and breeding. The same applies to dog racing, although to a lesser extent. The advent of satellite broadcasting technology has resulted in the development of so-called off-track betting facilities where bettors watch live telecasts at locations away from the racetrack.

There have been casinos or gambling houses since the 17th century, at least. Gambling became ubiquitous in the 20th century and took on almost a standardized appearance all over the world. Gambling is permitted in many or most holiday resorts in Europe and South America, but not always in cities. For many years, casinos in the United States have been legal only in Nevada and New Jersey and, by exclusive license, in Puerto Rico. Still, most other states also allow casino gambling, and betting facilities operate clandestinely across the country, often through the corruption of government authorities. Roulette is one of France and Monaco's leading gambling games in casinos and is popular around the world. At most American casinos, craps are the featured dice game. Slot and video poker machines are a centerpiece of casinos in the U.S. and Europe and are also found in thousands of private clubs, restaurants, and other ventures; they are also mundane in Australia. Among the casino card games, Baccarat, in its conventional form chemin de fer, remained a major gambling game in Britain and the most frequently patronized continental casinos at Deauville, Biarritz, and the resorts of the Riviera. Faro, once the United States' largest casino game, has become obsolete. Blackjack is an American casinos' main card game. In Monte-Carlo and a few other continental casinos, the French card game trente et quarante (or rouge et noir) is played. Many other games can be played in some casinos— sic bo, fan-tan, and pai-gow poker in Asia, for example, and local games like A Boule, Banque Francesa, and Kalooki in Europe.

Poker exploded in popularity at the beginning of the 21st century, mainly through the high visibility of televised poker tournaments and the abundance of playing facilities on the Internet. Another type of Internet gambling is the so-called betting exchanges— Internet websites where players make wagers with each other, with the website taking a small cut of each wager in return for the organization and handling of the transaction.

In a broad sense of the word, stock markets can also be considered a form of betting, albeit one in which the bettors play a considerable part by making use of their skill and knowledge. This also applies to insurance; in effect, paying the premium on one's life insurance is a bet that one will die within a specific period of time. If one wins (dies), the money of insurance is paid to one's family. If one loses (survives the time specified), the insurance company holds the wager (premium), which plays the role of a bookmaker and sets the chances (payout ratios) according to actuarial statistics. Such two forms of gambling, the former gaining venture capital, and the latter distributing statistical risks are considered beneficial to society.

Problem Gambling and Gambling Addiction Gambling problems can arise from any part of life. Your gambling ranges from a casual, harmless diversion to a harmful obsession with severe consequences. Whether you're betting on sports, scratch cards, Roulette, poker, or slots — at a casino, track, or online — a gambling issue may strain your relationships, interfere with work, and cause a financial catastrophe. You might even do stuff that you never thought you'd do, like running up huge debts or even stealing money to gamble.

Addiction to gambling is also known as pathological gambling, compulsive gambling, or gambling disorder. Thus it is an impulse-control disorder. If you're a compulsive gambler, even if it has negative consequences for you or your loved ones, you can't control the impulse to play. You're going to play whether you're up to or down, broke, or clean, and you're going to keep playing regardless of the consequences— even if you know the odds are against you or you can't afford to lose.

This book tries to unleash the myths and facts surrounding gambling while going through in detail its historical existence and how it has evolved over the years to attain its present form and types along with its widespread usage. Besides discussing various types of gambling, this book will also deliberate upon its symptoms, causes, its effects on individuals and society, and finally, ways and means to treat it successfully.

CHAPTER 2: Gambling and its History

2.1 What actually is gambling?

Let us first explore the different definitions of gambling and meanings ascribed to it as an activity by various authentic wordbook sources.

Cambridge Dictionary has this definition of gambling:

The activity of taking a risk in money on the result of something, such as a game or horse race, hoping to make money.

Collins describes gambling as:

The act of betting money, for example, in card games or on horse racing.

Oxford dictionary gives a precise definition of gambling in the following manner:

The activity of playing games of chance for money and of betting on horses, etc.

Princeton's Wordnet treats gambling as a noun describing it as:

The activity to play for support in the hope to win (which includes the chance to win a prize or payment of a price)

Finally, more concrete and relevant description of gambling is presented by Business Dictionary. It explicitly says:

Gambling is a special form of betting, which must result in either a gain or a loss. Gambling is not a taking of risk in the context of speculation (assumption of significant short-term risk) or an investment (acquisition of property or assets to achieve long-term capital gains). It also differs from policies that can reduce or eliminate the risk of loss, but does not provide a legitimate chance of benefit.

The overwhelming use of words such as risk, chance, and uncertainty clearly demonstrates the unpredictable nature of gambling concerning its result and thus allude to harmful and detrimental effects it can have on individuals, families, relationships, and society at large.

There has been a swift increase in the accessibility of legalized gambling in the United States and other parts of the world over the past several decades, and especially over the past 10 to 15 years. The associations between gambling patterns and health status have been extensively investigated by a few scientific studies. Existing data support the idea that certain gambling behaviors, particularly problem gambling and pathological gambling, are correlated with non-gambling health issues. Gambling is a very common illegal practice that can be considered a non-drug related behavior with an addictive-potential. In a general medical setting, the relative importance of assessing the gambling habits of patients depends in part on the associated health risks and benefits.

Are there different types of Gambling Addiction?

Gambling displays a variety of behaviors, so there are many different types of gambling addiction. When someone is addicted to gambling, deciphering, or ascertaining the addiction is not easy. The act of gambling is not confined to slot machines, cards, and casinos, contrary to popular belief. There are other available forms of gambling, such as buying a lottery ticket, entering a raffle, or making a bet with a friend.

Gambling addiction can arise when a person feels financially ruined and believes that they can only solve their problems by risking what little they have in an effort to get a large sum of money. Sadly, this almost always leads to a cycle where the gambler thinks he has to win back his losses, and the cycle continues until the person is forced to seek rehabilitation to break his habit.

Another type of addiction to gambling results in a gambler playing the games and making extremely risky bets just to experience the emotional high associated with taking huge risks that sometimes pay off. The person affected by this addiction must be willing to stop the behavior in both situations, not just to appease family and friends.

Problem Gambling and Pathological Gambling

Gambling can also be defined as placing something of value at risk in the hopes of gaining something of greater value. Wagering in casinos and lotteries, horse and dog racing, card games, and sporting events are common ways of gambling. Gambling is an extremely widespread activity, with 86 percent of the general adult population endorsing lifelong involvement in traditional forms of gambling and 52 percent of adults reporting active involvement in past-year lottery gambling.

Gambling issues can happen to anyone from any walk of life. Your gambling ranges from a fun, harmless diversion to an extreme, unhealthy obsession. Whether you're betting on sports, scratch cards, Roulette, poker, or slots — at a casino, track, or online — a gambling problem may strain your relationships, interfere with work and cause a financial catastrophe. You might even do stuff that you never thought you'd do, like running up huge debts or even stealing money to gamble.

Gambling addiction is an impulse-control disorder and is also known as pathological gambling, compulsive gambling, or gambling disorder. If you're a compulsive gambler, even if it has negative consequences for you or your loved ones, you can't control the temptation to play. You're going to play whether you're up to or down, broke, or clean, and you're going to keep playing regardless of the consequences— even if you know the odds are against you or you can't afford to lose.

Of course, without being totally out of control, you can also have a gambling problem. Any gambling activity that disrupts your life is a problem gambling. You may be suffering from a gambling issue if you are obsessed with gambling, wasting a major portion of your time and money on it, chasing losses, or gambling in spite of serious consequences in your life.

The addiction or problem with gambling is often associated with other disorders of behavior or mood. Many problem gamblers can also suffer from substance abuse issues, unmanaged ADHD, stress, depression, anxiety, or bipolar disorder. You will also need to tackle these and any other underlying causes to resolve your gambling issues.

While most people gamble, the criteria for a gambling disorder are met by a minority. Pathological gambling is the most extreme pattern of pathological or harmful gambling activity. It is the only gambling condition for which specific diagnostic criteria exist in the current American Psychiatric Association's (DSM-IV-TR) Diagnosis and Statistical Manual. In other words, problem gambling is often used to describe habits of excessive or harmful gambling that are less serious but disruptive, often inclusive, and sometimes exclusive of pathological gambling.

Pathological Gambling: An Addiction or Compulsion?

Two common, non-mutually exclusive pathological gambling conceptualizations identify the condition as an impulse control disorder located along an obsessive-compulsive spectrum or as drug addiction. Although data are available to support each categorization, broad proband trials of the obsessive-compulsive disorder have not typically reported increased rates of pathological gambling, nor have high rates of obsessive-compulsive disorder been identified in samples of the problem or pathological gamblers. The St. Louis Epidemiologic Catchment Area (ECA) study, for example, found an odds ratio of 0.6 in the problem or pathological gamblers, compared to non-gamblers, for obsessive-compulsive disorder. Compulsive traits, however, have long been defined as a core component of addiction. Current studies into the underlying neurobiologies are being undertaken to establish more accurately the correlation between "behavioral" dependency such as pathological gambling and addictions to drugs.

Gambling: Prevalence Rates

Prevalence rates of gambling activity and problem and pathological gambling have risen as a result of increasing legalized status of gambling opportunities. A meta-analysis of prevalence studies conducted over the past several decades found prevalence rates of 1.1 percent and 1.6 percent in adults, respectively, for pathological gambling and 2.8 percent and 3.8 percent for problem gambling, respectively. For primary care settings, similar or slightly higher rates were recorded (6.2 percent for one study), and consistently higher rates were found in other specific populations, including teenagers, persons in correctional facilities, and people with mental health problems.

2.2 A Brief History of Gambling

Gambling has been taking place, in some form or other, for hundreds if not thousands of years. From ancient China where traces of primitive games of chance were discovered on tiles to Egypt where the oldest known dice were digging out to scenes on Greek and Roman pottery showing that betting on animal fights was normal and animals would be bred for that sole purpose, humans love to play and do so at any opportunity.

About 200 BC' white pigeon ticket' was played in China's gambling houses with the local governor's approval, who would have earned a percentage of the profits, and the winnings were often used to finance state works; both Harvard and Yale were both initially funded by lottery money that they continue to use today.

It is believed that it was in the 9th century in China that playing cards first appeared, although the games played are unknown, and the cards have little resemblance to those used today. The cards were often adorned with human forms, but the Kings and Queens that we are more familiar with started to appear as games spread across Europe.

The Comprehensive History of Gambling

Human history is inextricably linked with gambling, as no matter how long you travel, there are indications that gambling is probably going on wherever groups of people come together. Now we're not going to try to track every single twist and turn on the evolution of gambling. However, we will select a few of the big dates to serve as benchmarks on the path to today's gaming adventure.

The Earliest Evidence of Gambling-2300bc

Although it is almost certain that certain types of betting have been very actively followed since the start of human civilization, the earliest concrete evidence comes from ancient China where tiles were found that seemed to have been used for a rudimentary game of chance. The Chinese' Book of Songs' refers to "the drawing of wood," indicating that the tiles actually should have been a part of a lottery-type game. There is ample evidence in the form of keno slips that were used as some lottery in about 200bc to finance state works–probably including the construction of China's Great Wall. Lotteries have continued throughout history to be used for public purposes–both Harvard and Yale have been founded using lottery funds–and continue to do so to this day.

Dicing on the Streets of Old Rome-500bc

The Greek poet Sophocles believed that dice were invented during Troy's siege by a mythological hero. While this may have somewhat questionable ground, his writings around 500bc were the first mention of dice in Greek history. We know that dice existed even earlier than this, as a pair had been unearthed from a 3000bc Egyptian tomb, but what's certain is that the ancient Greeks and Romans loved to play on all sorts of things, obviously at any given opportunity. In addition, within the ancient city of Rome, all forms of gambling-including dice games-were forbidden, and a fine levied on those caught was worth four times the bet. As a result, clever Roman people invented the first gambling chips, so they could claim to play only for chips and not for real money if they were nabbed by the guards. (Note that if you try at a Vegas casino, this ruse will not work).

Playing your Cards Right in China-800ad

Many scholars agree that in the 9th century, the first playing cards appeared in China, although the precise rules of the games for which they were used were lost in history. Many say that the tickets were both the game and the stake, such as today's children's trading card games, while other sources claim that the first packs of cards were Chinese domino paper types. The cards used at this time certainly had very little to do with the traditional 52 card decks that we know today.

Baccarat in Italy and France-1400s

The oldest game still played in casinos today is Baccarat's two-player card game, a variant of which was first mentioned when it spread from Italy to France as early as the 1400s. It took hundreds of years and various inventions to enter the game we know today, despite its early genesis. Although the game's various incarnations have come and gone, the standard version played in casinos all over the world came from Cuba to the U.S. through Britain, with a few changes to the rules along the way. While Baccarat is more of a spectator sport than a game, due to its popularity with high-rolling gamblers, it is a feature of just about every casino.

Blackjack through the Ages-.1600

Many believe the early blackjack was created out of a Spanish game named "ventiuno" (21) as the game was published by Don Quixote's writer in 1601. The inventors of chance games were seldom documented in the historical annals as they were with all these origin stories. The Spanish game of 21 of the 17th century is undoubtedly a clear progenitor of the modern game, and this genre has entered the United States with early European settlers. The term "blackjack" was a novelty in the United States and was related in the 1930s to special promotions in Nevada casinos 10 to 1 bets have been charged to draw new buyers if the game.

First Casinos in Italy-1638

In the early 17th century in Italy began to emerge the first gaming houses which could accurately be associated with casinos. In 1638, for example, in the context of the yearly carnival, the Ridotto was built in Venice in order to ensure a safe gambling atmosphere. In the 19th century, Casinos began to emerge in continental Europe, while U.S. gambling houses were in high demand in the same period. Damp boats that carry wealthy farmers and merchants up and down the Mississippi have been the venue for many informal activities like gambling. Today, as we talk about the casino, we prefer to see the Las Vegas Strip that rose out of the remnants of the American depression.

The Little Wheel in Paris-1796

As we are already informed, Roulette was developed in the Paris gambling houses where the players knew (ironically enough) the device we now refer to as the American Roulette wheel. This took another 50 years to complete the' American' edition, and millions of roulette players could be thankful for this. Roulette became mainstream over the 19th century and, when the famed Monte Carlo casino developed the single zero-shaped design, it expanded across Europe and throughout most of the world even if the Americans stayed by the initial double-zero wheels

Poker: Bust to Boom-1829

It's hard to pinpoint the exact roots of poker as poker seems organically to have evolved from different card games in many of these competitions over the decades and perhaps centuries. Some have poker roots from Persia in the 17th century, while others claim the game we know today was influenced by a French game called Poque. What we definitely know is that Joseph Crowell's English actor recorded a familiar game style in New Orleans in 1829, so it's just dated the same as the birth of poker. The increase in demand and popularity of the game was rather slower until the 70s saw the launch of the world poker tournaments. Moreover, the emergence of online poker and T.V. events that enabled viewers to see the hands of players really exploded. Since qualifying for and winning the 2003 World Poker Championship, amateur Chris Moneymaker encouraged everyone to imagine themselves as millionaires of the online poker business.

One-Armed Bandits Appear in New York-1891

The very first gambling system that was comparable to the slots which we hear of today was one that was built by Mr. Sittman and Mr. Pitt in New York. Charles Fey in

San Francisco invented the Liberty Bell machine around the same time. The system was much more realistic in that winnings could be controlled specifically and marked the start of the real slot game revolt. This dated back to this early innovation that some new video slot games still had bell signals. Whilst early machines distributed cigarettes and rubber rather than currency, cash-dispensing models quickly became a standard of bars and casinos around the world, and in 1976 the first video slot was created, paving the way for the following online video slots.

Gambling in the U.S.: Two Sides of the Same Coin- 1910

The U.S. has always had up-and-down connections regarding gambling since the very beginning of Western colonialism. When Puritan settler movements forbade gambling in their new settlements, emigrants from England found gambling much and were more than pleased to accept it. The dichotomous connection has remained unchanged until now, and public pressure in 1910 contributed to a national ban on playing gambling. Just like the ban of alcohol at the same moment, this was somewhat difficult to implement, and the game was marginally discreet. The fall of Wall Street and the Great

Depression in the early 1930s forced gambling to be allowed, as, for many, it had been the sole hope of alleviating their grinding poverty. While in many countries most popular in Las Vegas, Nevada, online gambling is legal today, however, it is still a gray area in the U.S. For now, several foreign internet casinos do not welcome American clients, but this will improve in the near future.

The New Frontier for Gambling-1994

Microgaming is among the world's largest creators of casinos and poker machines, and it is also a developer of web gambling. The leap into the world of real casinos was created in 1994, something like 2300bc on the Internet. In 5 years, online gambling amounts to over $1 billion, and today's industry is growing and multibillion dollars with over 1000 online casinos.

In 1996 the Kahnawake Gaming Commission was set up, which controlled online gaming operations and granted gambling licenses to many of the world's online casinos and poker rooms in the Mohawk territory of Kahnawake. This is an attempt to maintain fair and transparent the activities of registered online gambling firms.

Immediately after, the Internet Gambling Prohibition Act of 1999 had been passed, indicating that no online gambling service could be offered to any U.S. citizen. That hadn't applied. Online gaming for multi-players was also launched in 1999.

Playtech came in 2003 to the first live dealer casinos and brought us closer to a fusion between brick and mortar casinos and the virtual world.

Gambling Has Gone Mobile-2019

A new generation of players has brought technological advances. Evidence shows Web users are less likely to use the desktops and are more likely to use handheld devices. The same applies to those who like online gambling and enjoy playing on the go. The biggest gambling websites acknowledged the trend in use, and smartphone gambling now provides many more options.

Mobile devices are preferred to be useful for participants; players have immediate access to wagering opportunities and gambling, and on the same mobile platforms as operators understand that social networking is engaging with each other.

There is a rapid increase in people interested in it since New Jersey allowed online gambling in 2011. America has seen a drive to legalize it by state and the rapid increase in mobile gambling

The Future

It's as hard to predict the potential for gambling, as it's to discover some of the roots of today's gambling games. However, at the moment, a lot of attention is paid to the mobile gaming industry, where online casinos struggle to make games more compliant with recent handheld devices. The development of virtual reality is only taking the first steps as a business venture and you can be confident that gaming applications will take place. How would you like to sit down with a group of friends from all over the world at a virtual poker table, share some fun, try and tell if you're going to see a facial tick from home? Revolution. V.R. Headsets will make it happen perhaps not now, but definitely in some years' time if technology keeps advancing so rapidly.

Gambling on the Blockchain

Blockchain technology and cryptocurrency are transforming the gambling industry in respects that we hadn't yet dreamed a few years ago. It is becoming commonplace for casinos to use cryptocurrency for gaming and can be used as either the principal payment system or as an alternative to fiat-based payment systems. The Blockchain provides transparency, reduces the edge of the house, and reduces transaction costs. The Blockchain enables users to play freely and almost automatically withdrawal and deposit rates, so saving documentation or even building an account does not need to be handed over.

Blockchain technology has the same ability to play, enabling everybody to be a casino player. Although certain Bitcoin casinos allow users to finance casinos and gain from household share, they have been brought to the next stage through crypto platforms such as Ethereum, where ventures have created a system where token holders have separated automatically from the income that the Blockchain produces. Some create blockchain-based gaming technologies that allow casino operators with a zero-house edge, close-to-null transaction charges, and equal random numbers to develop and implement gaming applications.

There may be likely to become more advanced in this field, with developer teams introducing new gambling possibilities using blockchain technology.

Edgefund is one notion like that; Edgefund would create a joint bankroll that will enable approved players to create games that provide very significant payouts on the Edgefund site. Game promoters may offer fixed-odds games for themselves at zero financial risks, i.e., assured income for every bet they position. To do so, Edgefund must purchase the possibility from the game developers at the lowest mathematically confirmed expense to cover the central bankroll of the Edge Fund. This means that a rival intelligent contract cannot defeat Edge Fund and that game-operators cannot ruin themselves.

And then? Alright, nobody knows, but everything is possible when it comes to gambling.

Chances, Probabilities, and Odds in Gambling

Events or occurrences that are somewhat likely to occur in each case have equal opportunities. Every instance is completely independent in pure chance games; that is, every play has the same likelihood of achieving a given outcome as each of the other. In fact, assumptions of probability refer to a long-term series of events and occasions but not to single ones. The law of higher numbers is an expression of the fact that as the number of events increases, the ratios expected by probability statements become increasingly correct, but the absolute number of outcomes of a particular form departs from expectations with increasing frequency as the number of repetitions increases. It is the percentages that are reliable correctly, not the individual events or exact figures.

Among all possibilities, the likelihood of a favorable outcome can be expressed: probability (p) is equal to the total number of favorable outcomes (f) divided by the total number of possibilities (t), or p= f / t. But this applies only in luck-ruled cases. For example, in a two-dice tossing game, the final number of expected outcome is 36 (each of six sides of one die paired with each of six sides of the other) and the number of ways of creating, say, seven is six (made by tossing 01 and 06, 02 and 05, 03 and 04, 04 and 03, 05 and 02, or 06 and 01); thus, the likelihood of throwing a seven is 6/36 or 1/6.

It is common to represent the concept of possibility in terms of odds toward winning in most gambling games. This is actually the ratio of the desirable to the unfavorable possibilities. Because the possibility of throwing a seven is 1/6, on average, one in six throws would be advantageous, and five would not; thus, the chances of throwing a seven are 5 to 1. The possibility of getting heads in a coin toss is 1/2; the chances are one to one, sometimes called. Care must be taken to understand the expression on average, which most correctly refers to a greater number of cases and is not useful in individual cases. A common fallacy of gamblers called the maturity theory of chances (or the fallacy of Monte-Carlo), wrongly assumes that each game in a game of chance depends on the others and that a sequence of outcomes of one kind should be balanced by the other possibilities in the short run. Gamblers have developed a number of systems largely on the basis of this mistake; casino operators are delighted to promote the use of such systems and exploit the lack of the strict rules of chance and independent play by any gambler. Nevertheless, an interesting example of a game where each game relies on previous games is blackjack, where cards already used to deal from the dealing shoe influence the composition of the remaining cards; for example, if all the aces (value 1 or 11 points) were dealt, a "real" (a 21 with two cards) can no longer be accomplished. This assumption forms the basis for certain schemes where the house advantage can be overcome.

In some games, the dealer, the banker (the person collecting and redistributing the stakes), or some other player may have an advantage. Not all players, therefore, have equal chances of winning or equal payoffs. This inequality can be rectified by alternating between the players in the game positions. Nonetheless, commercial gambling operators typically make their profits by consistently holding an advantaged role as the dealer, or they charge money for the opportunity to play or deduct a proportion of the wagers on each game. In the dice game of craps— one of the big casino games providing the most favorable odds to the gambler— the casino returns to winners from 3/5 of 1 percent to 27 percent lower than the equal odds, depending on the type of bet made. Depending on the bet, the house advantage ("vigorous") for Roulette in American casinos ranges from about 5.26 to 7.89 percent and varies from 1.35 to 2.7 percent in European casinos. In the long run, the house always has to prevail. Some casinos also add rules that improve their earnings, especially rules that limit the sums that may be staked under certain circumstances.

Most gambling games contain, as well as chance, elements of physical ability or strategy. Like most other card games, the game of poker is a mixture of chance and strategy that also involves a great deal of psychology. Making a bet on horse racing or athletic contests involves evaluating the physical capacity of a contestant and using other assessment skills. For those gamblers who are sponsored by very few dealers and small if the players are assisted by a relatively large number of bettors, In order to ensure that chance plays a major role to decide the results of such activities, weights, disabilities or other corrective measures may be implemented in certain situations to give the players approximately equal opportunities to win, and changes should be made in the payoffs so that the probability of success and the severity of the payoffs are put in opposite proportion to each, For example, pari-mutuel pools in horse-race betting reflect different horses ' chances of winning as players anticipate. , the greater the option, the lower the individual payout. The same applies to bet on sports events with bookmakers (illegal in most of the U.S. but legal in England). Bookmakers typically take bets on the result of what is perceived to be an unequal match by allowing the side to be more likely to win to score more than a simple majority of points; this practice is known as setting a "point spread." For example, in a game of American or Canadian football, the more respected team would have to win, say, by more than 10 points. Give it is backing an even payout.

Sadly, in most gambling games, such processes can be interfered with to preserve the power of chance; cheating is possible and relatively straightforward. Much of the stress associated with gambling has been caused by some of its promoters and players ' dishonesty, and a large proportion of current gambling law is written for cheating regulation. Nevertheless, more regulations were tailored to governments ' attempts to extract tax revenue from gambling than to prevent cheating.

2.3 Types of Gambling

Gambling games can be classified into two groups, games dependent on chance, and games based on skills. Note, while luck plays a bigger role in games based on opportunity, it is an important force in games based on skill. For 100 percent accuracy, 100 percent of the time, game outcomes can never be expected in all types of legal gaming.

- Chance-based (100% contingent on chance)
- Skill-based (players have some control, but the chance remains an outcome factor)

Chance Based Gambling

Participants have no ability to change or influence the result of chance-based gambling, which is entirely dependent on random events.

Games / Activities:

Casino games:

- Slot machines
- Progressive bonuses
- Bingo
- Roulette
- Sic Bo
- Baccarat
- Lottery products:
- 50/50 raffles
- Pull-tabs
- Scratch'n win tickets
- 6/49
- BC/49

- Lotto Max
- Keno
- Pacific Hold 'em

Slot machine gambling is one of the most common forms of gambling dependent on chance. Game results are unpredictable in chance-based gambling games and are based entirely on random events. Teams have no way of influencing or impacting how the game ends and whether they win or lose their bet.

Chance-based gamblers may get into trouble, so they overestimate their degree of control over the game outcome. Most players are naming it opportunity. A person that knows they are fortunate or feels lucky will make decisions that they would not normally make when playing. It is crucial for chance-based gamblers to have a good understanding of how gambling actually functions, and to be mindful of prudent gambling techniques in order to keep gambling healthy and enjoyable.

Examples of Chance-Based Gambling

Casino and Community Gaming Center Games and Sports Slot machines Modern Bingo and Most table games (Roulette, sic bo, Baccarat, etc.) The pace or order of bets does not affect outcomes, nor does the player, venue, or table or system past, since each game is separate and random.

Lottery Products

- 50/50 raffles
- Pull-tabs
- Scratch'n win tickets

These products often provide set prizes that must be won individually.

Other Lottery Products

- 6/49
- BC/49
- Lotto Max
- Keno
- Pacific Hold 'em

Such lottery items can have awards split with multiple winners without winners or prizes. Prices can be fixed in advance or can be decided by selling tickets.

There are many types, locations, modes, and representations of gambling dependent on chance, but they all have one thing in common: all players have an equal chance of winning at all moments.

It is common to use the term ' chance' to apply to' likelihood' as in' what is the possibility that it will rain today? Luck' is often associated with' odds,'' randomness' and' probability.'

Skill-Based Gambling

In skill-based gambling, players can use betting strategies and techniques based on related knowledge or other players' decisions and behavior.

Games / Activities

Strategy, skill, knowledge, and chance

- Poker
- Blackjack
- Pai Gow
- Texas Shootout
- Horse Race Betting
- Sports Betting

Poker is the most popular type of skill-based gaming, where players compete with each other rather than the dealer in the room. Players benefit from prior experience playing the game in skill-based games. Techniques and tactics can be used, and some playing styles can be effective when playing the exact similar players more than once.

Nevertheless, it is important to remember that skill-based gambling is still gambling, so the outcome of the game is largely beyond the influence of each participant.

Poker players will overestimate their skill level and underestimate their opponents ' skill level. Players also get into trouble by misjudging the degree of control they have over the result of the game, as they have no power over what cards they are issued, what cards they are dealt with their opponents, and what choices their opponents may make.

Due to the unexpected outcome in all forms of gambling, particularly skill-based gambling, it is important to warn players about prudent gambling techniques in order to ensure that gambling remains a safe and fun game.

Examples of Skill Based Gambling

- Race and Sports Betting Activities
- Horse Race Betting

- Sports Betting
- Players use their experience for placing their bet on sport, celebrities, animals, etc.

For example, once a gamble is made, it is not necessary to affect the outcome, and it becomes the outcome of chance. For a fact, other bettors and bookmakers (bookmakers) use the same expertise to assess the payoff odds.

Casino Games / Activities

- Poker
- Blackjack
- Pai Gow
- Texas Shootout

Players can use betting strategies and techniques to try winning a hand or getting an advantage. Such tactics and methods may be focused on the behavior and action of other players for poker.

Strategies and tactics make it possible to monitor more participants than in mere chance games, but the consequences of wagers remain unpredictable. While strategies and techniques can help, there is no scheme that can be used to win every hand or eliminate the advantage of the house.

CHAPTER 3: Gambling: Myths. Psychology and Facts

No other practice associated with it has as many misconceptions as gambling. The volume of formally and informally spread misinformation is overwhelming. However, it has something to do with the luck-gambling relationship.

Superstitious people in a way that logical people don't believe in things this leads to the belief that there are many falsehoods that can devastate your bankroll.

Most of the public playing games often dislike math. Since gambling and luck are closely related, it should not shock anyone that gambling myths are similar to some basic math concepts.

Some Compulsive Gambling Myths and Facts Most people involved in recreational gambling don't think they might ever become addicted. After all, they only occasionally engage in gambling, never lose in one sitting more than a few hundred dollars, and always act responsibly.

Some people may not realize that until it's too late, their gambling habit has become an addiction. Here are some compulsive gambling myths that might surprise you.

Myth: Every day, compulsive gamblers are playing.

Fact: How often a person plays does not have a gambling addiction relationship. Pathological gamblers are only allowed to play once a week or once a month. It's the gambler's behaviors ' emotional and financial effects that signify an addiction.

Myth: When you lose every last penny, gambling becomes a problem.

Fact: A gambling addiction does not decide how much money you win or lose. Gamblers can win big and then lose all their earnings the next day, or they can gamble only a certain amount each time. Usually, gamblers will incur ample debt to start affecting their lives with the financial consequences of their actions, but this is not always the case.

Myth: Something like gambling can't get addicted.

Fact: Some activities are just as addictive as drinking or doing drugs, such as gambling. Gambling may create a euphoria that causes the player to continue to replicate the behavior in order to maintain this result. The gambler develops a desire for gambling, as with drugs and alcohol, and will take greater and greater risks to achieve this euphoria. A gambler can give into a gambling addiction by doing it more often, regardless of the negative consequences. Pathological gamblers, like any other addictions and compulsive behaviors, may also dispute their habits and may not believe they have trouble at all.

Myth: Compulsive gambling is merely a financial issue.

Fact: According to the National Council, compulsive gambling is an emotional problem with financial consequences. Even if the financial obligations of a gambler are taken care of, that person remains a compulsive gambler. The issue is not how much money the gambler has lost, but that the individual has an uncontrollable gambling addiction.

Myth: Even reckless people are gambling addicts.

Fact: It is common for people to assume that addicted people are weak-willed and reckless. But, no matter how responsible they are, anyone can become addicted to gambling. Once in their addiction, gamblers may indulge in risky activities to sustain their addiction.

Myth: The criminal behavior of all gamblers

Fact: Although some players may engage in criminal behavior, such as robbery or assault, this is not the norm. Often it's a sense of loss of control that drives a player to engage in such behaviors.

Myth: A gambler is going to bet on anything.

Fact: Gamblers usually prefer what they're going to be on and won't be tempted by betting on other issues. For example, lottery tickets or slot machines may not tempt a gambler who makes weekly trips to the race track.

Myth: If the gambler can afford it, compulsive gambling is not really a problem.

Fact: Just because people lose money doesn't mean their actions aren't problematic. Compulsive gambling usually interferes with all facets of the gambler's life, including family and friends and work relationships. The concern is the gambling conduct itself, not the financial effects of the crime.

Myth: This means paying off all their debts to help compulsive gamblers break their addiction.

Fact: The persistent bailing out of debt of a compulsive gambler can only make the conduct probable. Although getting the debt repaid may be a priority, treating the gambling addiction itself and getting the help needed to overcome the addiction is more important to the gambler.

Myth: A compulsive gambler is easy to recognize.

Fact: Unlike drug and alcohol addictions, there are very few obvious signs of compulsive gambling. The behavior is easy to hide from people, particularly if they are addicted to gambling.

If any of these myths are realities for you or a loved one, gambling addiction may need to be treated.

Many of the words that we use have origins in gambling. Think about how many times a day you start a phrase, "I bet..." Here are a few more examples:

The chances are

- It's a sure thing!
- It's a crapshoot.
- I've got an ace in the hole

It's a safe bet (another term from gambling) that you've used such phrases before! All these common words prove that gambling has been around for a long time— long enough to build a few myths. Here are a few other common gambling myths and facts.

Myth: Gambling is a means of making money.

Fact: Gambling is a way to lose money more often than not. If you're playing, think of it as something you've got to pay for, just like a movie or dinner with friends. That can help you keep playing in perspective— and if you end up winning any money now and then, it's going to be a nice treat instead of relying on something you've been.

Myth: People will tell if heads or tails of a coin toss would come up.

Fact: Each coin flip is a separate event. What happened in the previous flips doesn't matter. The probability of a single flip of heads or tails is 50 percent, regardless of how many times you turn the coin.

Myth: There are mechanisms that make winning lottery numbers easier to predict.

Fact: How you choose the numbers doesn't matter; your chances of winning are always the same. Take, for example, a lottery-like Lotto 6/49. All the numbers are mounted in a drum and mixed together. By chance, the range is perfect. The number has the same probability of being chosen (a 1 in 49 chance of being accurate). For one ticket, the odds of winning the jackpot are 1 in 13,983,816.

Myth: The majority of teenagers are not playing.

Fact: gambling for about 2 out of 3 teenagers

Myth: Teens are not having issues with gambling.

Fact: Teens tend to play with friends, not in casinos, but that doesn't mean that they can't have gambling issues. A 2008 study of Alberta students in grades 7 to 12 found signs of problem gambling, just over 2 percent, so about 2 out of every 100 students surveyed. Approximately 4 percent or 4 out of 100 students showed signs of risk of developing gambling problems.

Myth: When they have a losing streak, people can usually win back their money.

Fact: Not true, not true! Casinos remain in business because most people don't get back their money. Think about it: how long would a casino remain in business if it spent more money than it took in? The truth is that in these places, most gamblers lose much more money than they win.

Myth: Lottery winning will put you on "easy street."

Fact: You're not under the age of 18! In Alberta, purchasing lottery tickets, collecting lottery winnings, or playing any other game sponsored by the Alberta Gaming and Liquor Commission is against provincial lottery regulations for those under 18. (Including scratch-and-win tickets.) Some Pervasive Myths & Facts Myth: The more you're playing, the more likely you're going to have a big win.

Fact: Any gambling event's result is due to chance. Spending longer gambling has no impact on the outcome of the next game. This is known as the' event independence'-each outcome of an event (e.g., lottery draw or reel spin) is independent of those before or after. Given the edge of the house and return to the mechanics of the player mentioned above, a longer amount of time spent playing games would usually mean paying more for that leisure time.

Myth: You'll eventually win all of your money back if you keep playing for long enough.

Fact: The more you're playing, the more likely you're going to lose more money. The odds are always in favor of those offering the bet–the bookies, casinos and lottery companies know that some people are going to win, but more people are going to have to lose in order to keep the companies in the business.

Myth: A good knowledge of a game improves the chances of winning.

Fact: It's all down to chance, once again. Games like poker and sports betting can take advantage of extra knowledge, but you can't guess the outcome. You may think you're the best poker player in the world, but somebody else might be better or have stronger cards. The last two matches may have won your football team, but that doesn't mean they're going to win a third. Remember to play it safe at all times.

Myth: Keeping track of previous results when playing games can help you figure out the results to come.

Fact: When it comes to gambling, there is no pattern. If a pattern existed, it would all learn, and no one would ever lose. If no one was lost, there would be no money left in the slot machines, and the bookies and casinos would be bankrupt, and the winners could not be paid. Believing this will only make you lose a lot of cash and stop playing fun.

Myth: I've almost won; I've got to have a victory.

Fact: Winning "nearly" doesn't mean there's a real win around the corner. Future results of gambling are not influenced by previous results in any way.

Myth: I'm going to increase my chances of winning if I play more than one slot machine or in more than one poker game at a time.

Fact: Of course, by playing two slot machines or poker games at a time, you can win more often, but make no mistake about it: you'll also spend — and ultimately lose — more on it. Note, the more you play, the more you lose.

Myth: If I see a certain card regularly coming up in a poker game, I will bet on it because it's likely to come up again very soon.

Fact: In a 52-card deck, 2.6 million hands are possible. As each hand is independent of the last, there is no more (or less) probability that one card will come up again once it has already appeared than any other card.

Myth: I've got a special strategy to help me succeed. I pick a lottery number and press the stop button on a slot machine at the right time.

Fact: The outcome of most chance games, particularly lotteries and slot machines, is completely random: no matter what you do, you cannot influence it. It means that betting the same numbers each week will not help you win more than betting different numbers. For example, the odds of winning Lotto 6/49 are 1 in 14 million each time you play: no matter how many people have purchased tickets or how many numbers you play, the odds are the same, regardless.

Whether you win or not playing slot machines is based solely on the randomly drawn numbers created by the computer of the machine — numbers that decide the outcome of the game even before the reels stop. When you figure out what the outcome of the game is, pressing the stop button will speed up, but it won't affect what that outcome is in any way.

Myth: I feel like it's my lucky day today. I feel that I'm going to win.

Fact: The expectation, urge, or even need to win money has no effect whatsoever on the outcome of a chance game. The FacebookMore1 Myth: Gambling is not addictive.

Fact: The idea behind the misconception that gambling is not really addictive argues that gambling has no physical effect, such as alcohol and drugs. But that's not really valid–because you believe your body has nothing to do with the brain.

The U.S. has an awful record of mental illness identification. Because the way cancer or heart disease does not always come with physical symptoms, people think that mental sickness is somehow less of a disease than a physical illness.

This kind of backward thinking destroys lives and interferes with the chances that people have to get well.

Not every player gets addicted.

But it does not help anyone to say that gambling is really addictive.

Myth: You'll finally have to change your luck, and you'll start to win.

Fact: This is an example of the gambler's mistake of a mathematical concept. The theory is that past results will affect future outcomes somehow.

This is not true with most (not all) gambling activities.

Here's an example: somebody playing roulette sees the result is black four times in a row. She could make 1 of 2 hypotheses:

Black is hot and on the next spin is more likely to come up again.

Red is due, and the next spin is more likely to occur.

But the likelihood of getting a black or red result depends on how many red results there are relative to how many black outcomes there are.

Since there are still all 38 of the pockets on a roulette wheel–they don't go anywhere when you reach them–the likelihood has not changed.

That roulette wheel spin is a separate event. Previous outcomes will not affect future outcomes.

Blackjack is an exception because the deck's composition is different once a card is dealt with.

Myth: When you go to be lucky, you're psychic, and you learn.

Fact: The outcomes of gambling are randomly decided. No one has any form of supernatural ability to improve their chances of winning at casino games. But many people believe they know when they will be fortunate.

Trying to convince someone who thinks he's psychic that he can't predict the future is probably pointless. Though, if it were not included, it wouldn't be a good list of gambling myths.

Spend some time reading about James Randi, who has spent decades debunking psychics, to find out more about why paranormal phenomena are a bunch of hokum. His foundation has been offering $1 million to anyone who could demonstrate documented paranormal activity for over 50 years–particularly psychological ability.

No one ever participated, and over 1,000 people took part in the contest in a few years.

Myth: Casinos are pumping oxygen to keep you alive and playing games in the sun.

Fact: You should be told by some common sense that this is not valid. For a minute, think about it. When interacting with air, what is the greatest danger?

This makes things more flame-retardant.

It would be a fire hazard like no other to pump oxygen into a crowded casino with its heavy use of electricity and its large number of people who often smoke cigarettes.

The theory is probably derived from a book by Mario Puzo, Fools Die, in which a fictional casino called Xanadu pumped in oxygen. The problem is its fiction.

At The Hoaxes Museum, you can learn more about this story.

Myth: Count Cards are illegal.

Fact: A little thought clarifies the fallacy of this theory. How could thinking about a game while you're playing it be illegal? Unless you use some kind of tool to keep up with the count, all you do is worry about the game you're playing when you're counting cards.

By the way, casinos are all right with this story. We discourage the easiest way to count cards. They're actually going to take countermeasures if they think you're counting cards. On each hand, they could start shuffling the deck. Or they might ask you not to play blackjack games. If they're really sticklers, they could even permanently ban you from their casino.

But for counting cards, you cannot be charged or punished. It is not illegal.

Myth: Are Rigged Casino Games.

Fact: This theory is valid in a sense, but not the way most people think.

Those who are persuaded that casino games are rigged claim that the casino will change the game results arbitrarily whenever they feel like it.

Remember the Casablanca scene where Rick asks the croupier to land the ball on some result?

This is fiction.

That's not happening in real life. Imagine the chances of landing a roulette ball at will in one of 38 pockets.

This makes no sense.

Nevertheless, casino games are designed with math that benefits the player's casino. A gambler can win in the short run, but it is less likely than losing.

The casino is always going to win over the player in the long run.

This is because, at lower odds, the bets pay off than the odds of winning.

In our post about the house edge and how it works, you can learn more about this idea.

The math behind the edge of the house is why casinos need not rig their games. The math is rigged already.

Myth: Illegal online gaming

Fact: Too universal to be valid is this assertion. Applying to a whole country like the United States is even too common. The U.S. laws are a patchwork of federal, state, and local governments—each also has different rules.

In fact, online casino gambling has been legalized by three states in the US. The other 47 states have not legalized or regulated online casinos, but not all of them have book laws that specifically make the activity illegal.

Facilitating money transfers for illegal gambling purposes is illegal, but this is another practice from placing a bet.

And while online gambling is clearly illegal in many states in the United States, no one has ever been arrested or prosecuted on the Internet for playing slot machines or blackjack. Until now, enforcement efforts have concentrated on online gambling companies rather than players.

Myth: It's all joy.

Fact: Luck plays a part in gambling, but not necessarily in your way of thinking. A mathematician would think that luck in your expected results is just a short-term fluctuation. In the long run, things are even going to come out.

But the belief that the outcomes of gambling are based entirely on chance ignores the role that good decision-making plays in gambling winning.

Here's an example: Blackjack is a game wherein the math behind the game, your decisions play a clear role. Each way a hand is played has an expected value. Your job as a player is to select the highest expected value for the decision. You're playing with basic strategy when you do this on every possible stick.

The difference among a blackjack player who uses basic plan and one who only plays her hunches is the difference between 0.5% and 4% house edge.

What does your bankroll mean?

When you play for $50 a hand and get 60 hands an hour, you bring $3000 into practice every hour.

You're looking for a loss of $15 per hour if you expect to lose 0.5 percent of that action. That's casino entertainment that's relatively cheap.

But if you expect to lose 4 percent of that action, you see a $120 per hour loss. This is a relatively expensive casino entertainment.

So common sense tells you that if the bottom of the house is lower, the chances of going away from a winner are greater.

Myth: To get an advantage on your next bet, you can use patterns.

Fact: This theory is closely connected with the fallacy of the gamblers above. Here's how the thinking works: at a Jacks or Better video poker machine, you're watching a play. You see, he's only played for 2 hours, but twice he's already hit a royal flush.

You believe that the pattern is to pay jackpots more often than other games for that console.

That's not real, though.

On a Jacks or Better video poker game, the odds of winning a jackpot are still about 40,000 to 1. The previous results do not change the number of cards in the deck or the variations that you will see on your computer.

Trends are taking place in gambling games. They really happen all the time.

But in retrospect, they are only apparent.

Depending on a pattern you've seen in the past, you can't predict what will happen in the future.

Myth: Cold and/or hot slot machines.

Fact: This is closely linked to the patterns and gamblers' fallacy bullet points. Die lovers of hard slot machines won't believe this, but retrospectively slot machines only get hot or cold. Just because a game of slots has been running hot for an hour or two does not mean that it will continue to run shot in the future. It also doesn't mean that "being cold" is more likely.

Modern slot machines are operated by a random number generator (RNG) computer program. This is a computer program that produces numbers per second at a rate of thousands of numbers. If you push the "turn" button or pull the lever, at that millisecond, the RNG will stop at whatever number it counted.

This computer program is not working slowly enough to allow you to predict where it is in its count. There is no way to know if the game paid off a lot or not.

Every reel spin is a separate event. The outcomes of subsequent spins are not influenced by previous spins.

Myth: The choices made by other blackjack players influence your winning chances.

Fact: This is one of the blackjack's most common myths. It has several permutations.

Another example is the assumption that the odds are ruined by a player jumping in and out of games. There is anecdotal evidence from many players that things went well at the table until a certain player arrived. Then there is a boom! The dealer wins the whole time.

This is an example of selective memory that is better than most people realize. Just because something happens before something else doesn't mean there's a connection between cause and effect. Probably most people forget someone jumped into a game all the time and all the players started winning.

The more popular permutation is the assumption that everybody at the table is harmed by a player using a less than optimal strategy. She would take a coin, for example, that would have broken the table.

In fact, the other players at the table profit from their mistakes as often as they damage them. In the long run, it all grows.

In reality, bad players enable better blackjack games to be offered by casinos. If everyone using perfect basic strategy, casinos would change the conditions of the game to improve the players ' edge.

Myth: Gambling online is a threat to children.

Fact: Many spurious arguments against online gambling will be seen. One of these is that it places children at risk.

The fact is that most online casinos will not allow you to start playing games for real money until you have proven you are legally old enough to play. This may be 18 years old or 21 years old, depending on the casino and its jurisdiction.

Yet online casino stories that victimize kid's gamblers are unheard of.

Online gambling firms create a lot of money without targeting underage gamblers. Worldwide jurisdictions require that minors be protected from gambling as a precondition for obtaining an operating license.

Myth: Online casinos are used only for money laundering.

Fact: This is a fallacy promulgated by the UIGEA (Unlawful Internet Gambling Enforcement Act) supporters. This is a statute added in an attempt to curb offshore gaming to the Safe Ports Act.

Is there money laundering in online casinos?

Maybe!

But the way to launder money is easier and safer.

Money laundering usually works by using a predominantly cash-operating business. Paper trails are anathema to a money-laundering operation, like those provided by the use of credit cards and online wallets.

I have never seen any evidence that money is being laundered by online gambling companies.

Myth: The Loosest Slot Machines Are Near the Aisles.

Fact: This theory might have been accurate at one time. The idea is that casinos want to attract gamblers to play the slots. By bringing the loosest machines closer to the aisles where people walk, they're more likely to attract gamblers to the machines.

John Robison from American Casino Guide has explored these hypotheses with casino owners and slots operators. His inference from those discussions is that the changing nature of casinos and slot machines make it unnecessary to organize slot machines in this way.

The reality is that it is not possible to find slot machines with bigger payback percentages. Even though, if you do, you also need to compensate for variables like uncertainty and win duration. A progressive slot machine with a massive jackpot might have a high potential return, but the odds of winning the big jackpot—which makes up a healthy percentage of that return—are still astronomical.

Myth: It's Impossible to Beat the Casino in the Long Run.

Fact: Most of the myths listed the point at misconceptions linked to beating the casinos.

But few people are convinced that it is not possible to beat the casino in the long run.

And that's just not real.

Many games are mathematically unbeatable. These include games like slots and roulette.

Other games are beatable by seasoned advantage gamblers, such as video poker and blackjack.

Different techniques will allow a player to gain a statistical advantage over the house, ensuring that the player can beat the casino in the long run. Counting blackjack cards is just one example of a method of advantage gambling. It's another thing to combine video poker pay tables expertise with great strategy and rebates.

Of course, by just getting lucky and stopping gambling while you're ahead, it's also possible to beat the casino in the long run.

But where is that fun?

Myth: Playing with your inserted slots club impacts your winning chances.

Fact: I explained how a random number generator works in a slot machine in an earlier bullet point. This computer program is not linked to your club card slots.

If you think about it, you will know that there is no reason for the casino to penalize players for using their club card slots. The whole point is by giving them incentives to encourage gamblers to play more.

Why are you trying to do the opposite?

The only thing that plays with your inserted slots club is to track how much money you run through the machine. The more time you spend on a slot machine and the more spins you make, the more lucrative it will be for the casino.

Casinos don't mind winners on the slot machine from time to time. The occasional wins behind the machine are already factored into the math.

The only goal of the casinos is to allow you to spend more time playing when it comes to slot machines and slot memberships.

Myth: The Casino can beat the Martingale System.

Fact: This one has some truth. Using the Martingale Method, you can often earn small wins in the short run.

The concern is that a huge loss would eventually wipe out these small wins.

Here's how the Martingale Model works in theory: you bet again each time you lose a bet, doubling your bet size.

You will eventually win, recover your losses, and end up with a one-unit profit.

Here's an example: at the roulette table, a Martingale player bets on black. He's betting and losing $20. He's betting $40 on the next spin and losing again. He bets $80 on the third spin and loses. He's won back the $50 he lost on the previous two spins, and for his efforts, he's got $20 income.

The Martingale Model has two big problems: it assumes you have an infinite bankroll.

It's saying you can bet as much as you like.

In fact, you have to bet with a finite amount of money.

And even if you have a huge bankroll, you will eventually hit a winning streak where the next bet is more than the table's betting limits.

Here is an example of a Martingale progression: $20 $40 $80 $160 $320 $640 If you're betting at a table with a

$500 max bet, you're only going to have to lose five times in a row before you can't keep going.

And you've lost $620 at that point.

You also lose $640 by the 6th bet to get a net profit of just $20.

Yes, the loss of 5 or 6 bets in a row is unlikely. But as you might imagine, it's not as unlikely.

Myth: On a slot machine, pulling the lever is more likely to produce a win than clicking the button "Spin."

Fact: I discussed how the random number generator on a slot machine functions in the post a few times, but for more clarification: the random number generator doesn't know whether you pulled the lever or pressed the "spin" button.

It lands on the number when you hit the button or pull the lever that you are talking about.

Moreover, what reason for such a discrepancy would the casino have?

That one just doesn't make sense. It's plain and simple superstition.

Myth: Casinos can adjust the results of the game if you have won too much.

Fact: Casinos need not adjust the outcomes of their games. All of their games already come with an integrated edge of mathematical houses that cannot beat in the long run. This is similar to the myth that a roulette wheel spin results can be controlled by the croupier.

Sometimes players win in the short run because that's the nature of likelihood. There is likely to be short-term volatility.

Casinos, on the other hand, deal almost instantly with long-term figures.

An average player is making 600 spins in an hour on a slot machine. Even if she plays four hours a day, only 2400 spins have been generated, which is statistically insignificant.

But a casino with 1000 slot machines running 24 hours a day may see 24,000 X 600 spins, or 14.4 million spins a day. Even though those games are empty 50 percent of the time on average, that's still 7 million spins a day.

Once you reach the millions of spins, you will begin to see outcomes that are close to statistical standards.

Multiply the number of spins by 30 days a month or 365 days a year, and you can easily see how the long-term casino is operating.

Because the math behind these slots games ensures a 4 percent or more long-term winnings expectation, the casino stands to make plenty of money without ever having to worry about fixing the results on their games.

The same method of thinking also applies to other casino games.

For individual players, casinos simply don't need to micromanage the results of individual games.

Myth: Bookmakers once they occur, they know the results of events.

Fact: In this post, I haven't delved into too many sports betting myths, because I'm more of casino games and poker expert.

But it's too easy to debunk this theory.

When bookmakers knew before they occurred the consequences of each case, they would be far more successful than they are. They would not have to change the lines, either, depending on the behavior of the public. They would just be sending out the lines and odds to maximize their benefit.

Bookmaking is the only way to think about it as a market, like the stock market. Based on how attractive they are for betters, lines and odds are adjusted. If a game has too much action on one side, the bookmakers will adjust their lines to try to even out the action on both sides.

They wouldn't have to do that if they knew the outcome beforehand. They would just make sure on the opposite side of the assured winner they had as much action as possible.

When determining the point spread, bookmakers are remarkably accurate. The upsets happen every week, though.

Even the Cleveland Browns win a game of football from time to time.

Myth: tickets from BC/49 are more likely to win than tickets from Lotto 6/49 because fewer people are playing because they are only available in BC.

Fact: The Lotto 6/49 winning chances are based on possible combinations of numbers, not the number of tickets sold. The matching odds of 6/6 numbers are 1 in 13,983,816. Similarly, the odds of winning BC/49 are based on possible combinations of numbers and are exactly the same as Lotto 6/49: one in 13,983,816.

Myth: "I feel lucky." or "My lucky charm will help me win."

Fact: I can't use luck to predict what's going to happen in the future. When people believe in luck, they will realize that the most common luck faced by gamblers is bad luck when it comes to gambling. Gambling outcomes are unpredictable, and gambling is risky behavior.

Myth: For a big jackpot, some slot machines are hot.

Fact: BC slots pay 92 percent of all wagered money on average. Nevertheless, the payout rate is based on a machine's life, not on one session of play. The laws of probability would encourage many players to win and cause many more to lose over the life of a slot machine or put another way, after millions and millions of spins. The truth is that slot machines have Random Number Generators (RNGs) inside them to ensure that a random result is generated by each spin. A computer is as likely to have winning combinations and big payouts back-to-back as it is to have losing combinations and defeats back-to-back.

Myth: "I will learn a system that will overcome the odds."

Fact: there is no system that you can use to overcome the advantage or odds of the house. In reality, many such systems are designed to enable gamblers to bet more money than they should otherwise because they create a false sense of the potential ability of the gambler to win using the program. Many such devices that are sold to gamblers are simply designed to encourage gamblers to play even more money-allowing the player to lose more money more quickly. Each game has a random element that cannot be overcome. This is a requisite gambling condition.

Myth: "I win more at slots because I'm playing the Max Bet!"

Fact: it's true that for many slot machines if the wager made before the spin was the highest permissible (or greater than the lowest), the big win payout at better odds. Nonetheless, the average player return (ARP) still in the region of 92 percent. And essentially, when you encounter big wins, you just notice the difference, which doesn't happen very often. While you pay more to play, which increases the pace, you lose your money.

Myth: "The more I practice, the better I get."

Fact: Training is not optimal with gambling. One play doesn't affect another, and there's no system or way of winning. Note, every game has an element of chance that even with practice can't be overcome. Playing poker or betting on sports can take some skill, but these games still involve chance. You're more likely to lose over time than to win.

Myth: "Gambling.net pages are harmless and fun since there is no bet on money."

Fact: While it is true that.net sites do not require you to play money, it is important to understand that they are designed specifically to guide you to.com (pay) sites.

Practice (.net) sites make it easier for you to succeed, contributing to a false sense of competence and power.

It makes the.net pages especially dangerous for children and young people. When false assumptions are formed about one's chances, skills, or ability to win at gambling, they are difficult to overcome. False beliefs can lead to bad gambling habits and bad decision-making.

Myth: "I'm great at computer games, so I'm sure I'm going to be good at internet poker." Reality: gambling is risk-based and chance-based. The skill involved in video games has nothing to do with any kind of gambling.

Even a gambling-based video game is unlikely to have the same chances and rewards in the real world that a player will face.

Myth: "I'm going to beat everyone at bingo because I'm playing multiple cards!" Fact: with the number of cards a person plays, the chances of winning in bingo are growing, but so are the costs of playing. Most people accept this additional cost because they feel it is a significant advantage to do so. The real benefit of playing multiple bingo cards is less than expected.

Say, for instance, there are 100 cards in play. If you play five bingo cards instead of a single card, your odds go from 1-in-100 to 5-in-100. Note, though, the cost of playing has also risen five times, so you're investing your betting money five times faster, and in each bingo round, you're still likely to lose 95 out of 100 times.

The reality is that, no matter how many cards you play, the house advantage remains constant.

Myth: The problem of gambling does not affect children.

Fact: Research shows that about 10% to 15% of American and Canadian adolescents have encountered gambling-related issues and 1% to 6% of those individuals that meet diagnostic criteria for pathological gambling. In fact, it has been shown that children from problem gamblers are at a higher risk of developing health-related habits. It includes drug and alcohol use, gambling problems, eating disorders, depression, and suicide.

Myth: Problem gamblers' partners often drive problem gamblers to play games.

Fact: Problem gamblers are able to find ways to streamline their gambling. Blaming others is a way to avoid taking responsibility for actions, even steps necessary to overcome the issue of gambling.

Myth: Financial issues are the main reason why the relationships of problem gamblers break down.

Fact: It's true that money issues play a major role in ending marriages, but many non-gambling partners claim that the biggest cause is lies and lack of trust.

Myth: Problem gamblers' parents are to blame for the actions of their children.

Fact: Most issue gamblers' parents feel hurt and bad about the gambling actions of their son or daughter, and they are not to accept responsibility.

Myth: If a problem gambler creates a debt, the important thing to do is to help them get out as soon as possible of the financial problem.

Fact: Quick fix strategies are often appealing to everyone engaged and may seem the right thing to do, since "bailing" the gambler out of debt can actually make things worse by allowing gambling issues to continue.

Myth: It's easy to recognize problem gambling.

Fact: Secret addiction was called problem gambling. It's very easy to hide because, unlike alcohol and drug use, it has little noticeable effects. Most problem gamblers do not know that they have a problem with gambling. Problem gamblers also devote themselves to self-denial.

Chances, Myths, and Evidence

What are your chances? The odds are against you!

Do you know about the odds are of actually winning if you play for the chance to win money? The odds against the gambler are clearly stacked–that is, you should always expect to lose.

The odds are against the player in each betting game. Many people may not realize the true probability of statistics that will guarantee that they lose money over time.

Remember:

- Chances are always against the better
- The' home' always has the advantage, the' edge
'• The more you play, the more often you lose than you win.

Winning chances on' Pokies ' Pokies are expected to pay less than you put in them, so you'll lose the odds. Through chance, poker machines are completely affected–that is, there is no way of knowing what the result will be. The more you're playing on a poker machine, the more likely you're going to lose.

The winner is always the poker machine. Myth: "I know that if I hit the button on the console at the right time, I can stop the reels at a powerful combination" Fact: Gaming machines are using software running a Random Number Generator (RNG). The RNG runs through numbers continuously. The RNG selects a combination at random at that specified microsecond when you press the play button. After this initial press, anything you do will have no impact on the outcome of the game.

Myth: "The individual who played the game after I won big I should have kept playing because that win was mine" Fact: any combination created by the gaming machine is completely random. This means that you cannot predict the next winning combination on a console. That spin is a random occurrence that has no impact on what has happened or is about to happen before.

Myth: "My gaming machine hasn't paid out for a while, so it's due to winning" Fact: a game's result is random and unpredictable. You can win the next spin, or you can lose the next one. It's completely random.

Myth: "When you bet in a certain pattern, you're more likely to win" Fact: each game's outcome is completely random.

Myth: "When I cash out after each win, my chance of winning will improve" Fact: A player who cashes out after each win has the same chance of winning as a player who does not cash out. Cashing out doesn't affect the outcome of the game.

Myth: "Some poker machines are luckier than others" Fact: -poker machine is just a computer programmed to produce random results.

Myth: "Gaming machines appear to pay out higher or more often at certain times of the day" Fact: All games outcome is random. Combinations that win or lose are not correlated with clocks or calendars.

Winning prospects on some forms of gambling in South Australia • Poker machines Winning 5 Black Rhinos on Black Rhinos Game (Top Prize) ($1 bet per line) Winning chances-1 in 9,765,625 • Lotto Winning First Division (playing 1 game) Winning chances-1 in 8,145,060 • Oz Lotto Winning First Division (playing 1 game) Winning chances-1 in 45,379,620 • Powerball Winning First Division (playing 1 game)

Winning Odds Compared to Non-Gambling Related Activities

- Chances of experiencing depression in your lifetime ^-1 in 7 people

- Chances of having mental illness each year-if you are a young Australian-1 in 4 people

- Marriage ending in divorce-1 in 2.3 marriages

- Chances of a man going bald-3 in 4 men

- Death from heart disease-1 in 4 people

- Stolen your car-1 in 4 people

- I've listed 20 of the most popular and fascinating gambling myths, but without too much effort, you can become able to come up with a list of another 20.

Although stopping gambling can sound like you're helpless, there are plenty of things you can do to solve the issue, restore your relationships and finances, and eventually regain control over your life.

Gambler's Psychology Gambling is an interesting social trend, and extensive research has been done on how gambling activity is influenced by psychological processes. Here are some interesting phenomena of gambling.

A recent study found a link between things that cause a positive mood (# of sunny days; local sports teams ' success) and increased gambling. The theory was that more risk-taking benefits from a positive mood.

Gambler's fallacy So, when 7 black numbers come up in a row, a roulette player watches, so he puts all his money on red. This well-known psychological process is called the fallacy of the gambler and is the mistaken belief that a particular occurrence is inevitable if an event occurs frequently. In fact, there are always the same chances of any particular event occurring.

Shifting expectations of winning, in a clever test, racetrack bettors were asked to measure the chances of winning their favorite horse pre and post betting on the horse. Gamblers appeared to assume that their horses had a greater chance of winning after making their bets than they had before betting. We were more optimistic because of the increased effort.

If lottery jackpots hit record levels and attract a lot of media attention, there's a frenzy of buying tickets when people decide they don't want to be left out of the loop. Even people who have never played the lottery before at these times will "jump on the bandwagon" and purchase some tickets.

By its very nature, gambling structures and superstitions Gambling is a random event. However, many gamblers firmly believe they can build a winning gambling scheme. It involves trying to predict trends in random numbers (there are no), choosing "hot" slot machines and avoiding "cold" ones (e.g., continuing to play a machine because it's "hot;" playing a machine that has not paid off in a long time, believing it's "due"), or performing some ritualistic activity to keep winning (I know of several gamblers who hit slot machines with a lucrative one).

Gambling can be incredibly addictive, as you know, and often these psychological processes work to intensify the addiction. Studies in neuroscience showed that addiction to gambling has many of the same neural processes as an addiction to drugs.

The best way to break an addiction to gambling is by breaking down gambling mistakes and learning how to handle addiction. There are a lot of good websites and hotlines, including the National Council on Problem Gambling, to help deal with gambling addiction.

The National Council on Welfare (1996) analyzed the findings of eight Canadian adult prevalence studies in an attempt to identify a problem gambler's profile as described by other studies of the male gender. The study found a fairly consistent trend between male, single, and under the age of 30 years of problem gambling. Young adults (18-24 years of age) were nearly twice as likely to have moderate to serious gambling problems in the Ontario prevalence study as the general population (7% vs. 3.8%).

Similarly, Korn (2000) found in his study of prevalence studies that being white, young, and having concurrent substance abuse or mental illness put people at higher risk for gambling-related issues.

Financial restrictions In the NORC report (1999), problem gamblers were more likely to be on social assistance than non-problem gamblers, declared unemployment, had mental illness problems, sought mental health care in the previous year, and were convicted or incarcerated.

Race, age, and parental background Volberg and Abbott (1994) found that race, sex, parental history (a parent with a gambling problem), marital status, and household size were the variables that most discriminated between the coupled problem-pathological and non-problem classes.

Emotional Factors and Depression A number of studies directly explored the relationship between emotional states and levels of gambling (Jacobs, 1986; 1987; Rosental, 1993). Nonetheless, because this work appears to focus on cross-sectional designs, it is difficult to establish with any precision the temporal sequence of gambling and various emotional indicators. McCormick et al. (1984) explored the association between diagnosable influence and pathological gambling disorders. The sample consisted of 50 admitted pathological gamblers to an inpatient treatment program for gambling. Of the overall study, there was a major depressive disorder in 38 patients (76 percent). An interesting question, as noted by the authors, is whether depression creates inspiration to escape this feeling via gambling or whether the losses of gambling create depression. Participants in the study group were unable to reliably report the temporal relationship between early gambling and early episodes of depression.

Beaudoin and Cox (1999) looked at the characteristics of 57 adults looking for gambling issues treatment. Around 30% of the sample in the past reported receiving mental health services, most usually for depression. In addition, gambling was reported by 40 percent of the sample to rid unpleasant feelings. Such results suggest that gambling can serve as a tool for dealing with depression for some people. Pathological gambling is often associated with other behavioral problems, including the misuse of drugs, mood disorders, and personality disorders (Blaszczynsk & Steele, 1998; NORC, 1999).

Co-morbidity-Depression and depression

An important yet complicating element in the evaluation of the cause of this condition is the shared occurrence of two or more medical disorders, called co-morbidity. Is issue or pathological gambling a particular disorder that occurs alone, or is it merely a symptom of a social predisposition that underlies all addictions, hereditary or otherwise? Recently, the Manitoba Addictions Foundation's extensive longitudinal and open-ended interviews with problem gambling clients found that, in addition to depressive feelings, many problem gamblers reported playing in bars and casinos to relieve their intense sense of loneliness. A study of women with gambling problems by Brown 6and Conventry (1997) found that women's gambling motivations were boredom, depression, and isolation. Trevorrow and Moore (1998) found that women who had gambling problems were significantly loner (more distanced) than non-gamblers and non-problem gamblers. Researchers conclude that their study is "suggestive of loneliness (or alienation) as either a consequence or a weakness factor in problem gambling, but it would require a longitudinal research design to explain this question" (Trevorrow and Moore, 1998: 263).

Adverse Life Experiences Stressors in life were also described as an important component in gambling problem growth. The General Theory of Addictions (Jacobs, 1986) indicates that certain aspects of personality and life events affect the development of gambling issues. Jacobs argues that a history of adverse childhood experiences may lead to excessive gambling. In addition, some scholars have correlated psychological insecurity with negative experiences of inadequacy, inferiority, low self-esteem, and rejection in childhood (McCormick et al., 1987; McCormick et al., 1989). Research by Taber et al. (1987) found that 23 percent of the 44 admitted to an inpatient gambling treatment program had experienced severe trauma during their lifetime, and another 16 percent had reported moderately severe trauma. In addition, those with traumatic experiences have reported higher rates of drug abuse, depression, and anxiety relative to those without these experiences.

Social Factors Strong or weak networks of social support may improve recovery or an addiction to gambling. Addiction research has found some of the protective factors against addiction to be strong family or friendship ties and the general presence of family and friends in the life of the affected person (AADAC, 2001). The present research adds to the limited knowledge available by using a longitudinal design to track health and adjust the level of gambling problems over a span of one year. The research also offers detailed information on the general population's relationship between depression, anxiety, isolation, life events, and levels of social support and gambling.

Identical Psychological and Social Patterns A study revealed the effect of psychological, social, and environmental influences on gambling problems: Psychological Influences / Feelings Lack self-confidence Drug abuse Male gender Social Factors Family risk.

Environmental Factors

Media advertising Gambling venues are available. These factors have contributed to problem gambling among high school students in Addis Ababa, Ethiopia. Global gambling studies show similar risk factors for problem gambling, including male gender, risk looking for patterns, low self-esteem, depression and suicide ideation; social factors like peer pressures and parental gambling; and environmental factors such as gambling ads have been found to be positively correlated with problematic gambling spectrum.

Additionally, the study explored various types of adolescents engaged in gambling activities. Research findings revealed that playing cards, flipping coins, pool gambling, and PlayStation are the most frequently played gambling types among high school students, whereas Internet gambling is one of the least recorded.

In their analysis of adolescent gambling in the Australian Capital Territory (ACT) of students aged 7 to 12 years, Delfabbro et al. (2005) revealed that private card games (39.8%) and bingo/scratchies (40.5%) were the most commonly reported gambling activities whereas betting on racing and sporting events were also common (32% and 26% respectively). In some other study conducted between many teenagers in Oregon (Carlson and Moore, 1998), buying raffle tickets (41%) was the most frequently cited gambling practice, followed by betting on sports of friends or relatives (32%); playing cards (31%) and betting on skill games such as pool or bowling (25%).

Adolescent Gambling Addiction Factors: A Bio-Psychosocial Approach Adolescent gambling addiction has often been referred to as "secret addiction" because:

• No visible signs or symptoms such as other addictions (e.g., alcoholism, heroin addiction, etc.)

• Money scarcity and debts can be easily explained in a materialistic society

• Adolescent gamblers do not feel that they are addicted.

Addictions are always the product of experience and interplay between many variables, including the biological and/or genetic predisposition of the individual, their psychological state, their social environment, and the very nature of the behavior. Gambling is not a single trend, but a multifaceted phenomenon. Consequently, in many ways and at different levels of study (e.g., biological, social, or psychological), several factors can come into play. Central to the new theory is that no single degree of study is considered adequate to clarify either the gambling behavior's etiology or maintenance. In addition, this view states that all work is context-bound and should be examined from a viewpoint that is mixed or bio-psychosocial. Variations in gamblers ' attitudes and features and in gambling behaviors themselves indicate that results in one setting are unlikely to be important or true in another.

Structure of Gambling Activities The structure of gambling activities is another key factor In understanding gambling activity. Gambling behaviors have been shown to vary significantly in their structural characteristics such as the likelihood of winning, the amount of gambler participation, the use of close wins, the amount of skill that can be applied, the duration of the stake-outcome period, and the extent of possible wins. Structural variations are also found in certain groups of activities such as slot machines, where discrepancies in the frequency of reinforcement, colors, sound effects, and features of machines may significantly influence the machine's usability and attractiveness. Each of these structural features (and almost certainly does) has consequences for the motives of gamblers and gambling habits ' possible "addictively."

Duration The duration of the game is another essential structural aspect of gambling, namely, the length of the stake-outcome interval. Continuous behaviors (e.g., cycling, slot machines, and casino games) with a higher play rate have been found to be more likely to be correlated with gambling issues in almost all studies. In short time periods, the ability to make regular stakes increases the amount of money that might be lost and also increases the likelihood that gamblers will not be able to control spending. These issues are seldom found in non-continuous operations, such as weekly or biweekly lotteries, where gambling happens less regularly, and results are often uncertain for days. Therefore, it is significant to recognize that if the expanded operations are continuous rather than non-continuous, the overall social and economic effect of the growth of the gambling industry will be significantly greater. Other structural factors and dimensions reported in the overall gambling literature (external to the person itself) include:

- Stake size (including affordability issues, perceived value for money)

- Event frequency (i.e., the time gap between each game)

Amount of money earned in a given time period (important in chasing); reward systems (i.e., number and amount of prizes)

- Probability of winning 1 in 14 million on a 6/49 lottery
- Jackpot size over £ 1 million on a lottery
- Skill and pseudo-skill elements real or perceived
- "Near miss" opportunities (number of near winning positions)
- Light and light effects (e.g., u.

Each of these discrepancies can have consequences for the motives of an adolescent gambler and the social impact of gambling as a result. It /must be noted, but that many of these structural characteristics that cause gambling are dependent on single factors such as biological/genetic predispositions and personality factors.

Situational characteristics

The situational characteristics of gambling behaviors are other aspects that are central to understanding gambling activity. These are the factors that often make playing in the first place simpler and encouraging people. Situational features are mainly environmental features (e.g., accessibility factors such as location of the gambling venue, number of locations in a specified area and potential membership requirements) but may also include internal features of the venue itself (decoration, heating, lighting, color, background music, floor layout, refreshment facilities) or encouraging factors that may be relevant to the situation. In both the initial decision to play and the maintenance of the actions, these variables may be significant. Although many of these situational characteristics are assumed to affect susceptible gamblers, very little empirical work has been done on these factors and more research is needed before any conclusive conclusions can be drawn on the direct or indirect effect on gambling activity and whether vulnerable individuals are more likely to be influenced by these specific types of ma

One consequence of the recent rise in adolescent gambling research is that we can now begin to put together a "risk factor model" of those individuals who may be at the greatest risk of developing addictive gambling trends. A number of specific risk factors appear in the creation of problem adolescent gambling based on the previous description and empirical research literature summaries. Adolescent problem gamblers are more likely to:

- Be male (16–25 years of age)
- Have started gambling at an early age (as young as 8 years of age)
- Have had an earlier major win in their gambling careers
- Consistently chase losses
- Have started gambling with or alone with their parents
- Be anxious before gambling
- Be nervous and excited during gambling
- Be irrational (i.e., have misperceptions)

This list is not exhaustive but includes what is known empirically and anecdotally about gambling for adolescent issues. In addition, many of the risk factors involved in adolescent problem gambling have been believed to be very close to the risk factors involved in adolescent drug abuse (i.e., family history, low self-esteem, depression, history of abuse, etc.).

Although a change of personality has been recorded in young gamblers, many parents may attribute the change to adolescence itself (i.e., evasive behavior, mood swings, etc. are commonly associated with adolescence). This is quite often the case that, once their son or daughter is in trouble with the police, many parents do not even know they have a problem. There are a number of possible signs of alarm to watch for, although many of these symptoms could be put down to puberty on an individual basis. However, if some of them apply to a child or adolescent, they might have a problem with gambling. The symptoms include:

A sudden decrease in the quality of schoolwork

- Going out every night and being evasive about where they were

- Mood changes such as being sullen, moody, or always on the defensive • Money missing from home

- Selling costly things and not being able to account for the money

- Loss of interest in hobbies they used to love

- Lack of concentration

CHAPTER 4: Problem and Compulsive Gambling: Signs, Symptoms, and Causes

Problem Gambling or Compulsive Gambling or Impulse Control Disorder

Gambling is harmless fun for many people, but it can turn into an issue. This form of compulsive behavior is often referred to as "problem gambling." A gambling problem is a progressive addiction that can have a lot of negative psychological, physical, and social effects. It is in the Diagnostic and Statistical Manual of the American Psychiatric Association (APA), fifth edition (DSM-5). Psychological and physical wellbeing is detrimental to problem gambling. People living with this addiction may experience depression, migraine, nausea, intestinal disorders, and other problems associated with anxiety.

The effects of gambling, as with other addictions, can lead to feelings of disappointment and hopelessness. In some cases, this may lead to suicide attempts.

Gambling addiction has become a major public health issue in many countries due to its harmful consequences.

Gambling addiction is a psychological-health problem that is known to be one of many types of problems of impulse-control and many similarities to obsessive personality disorder. Nonetheless, being more common to other addictive disorders is now known. The forms of gambling that could involve people with this condition are as complex as the available games. Betting on football, buying lottery tickets, playing poker, slot machines, or roulette are just a few of the compulsive gamblers ' habits. The place of choice for people with a gambling addiction also varies. While many prefer gambling in a casino, with the increasing use of the Internet, the online / Internet gambling addiction rate continues to rise. Conversely, certain compulsive players may also make risky investments in the stock market. Addiction to gambling is known as compulsive gambling or pathological gambling.

Problem Gambling as an addiction is a crippling condition that causes depression and anxiety.

The sensation of gambling is equivalent to taking a drug or having a drink for someone with a gambling addiction. Gambling behavior changes the mood and state of mind of the person. We keep repeating the behavior as the individual becomes accustomed to this feeling, trying to achieve the same effect.

For example, the individual begins to develop tolerance in other addictions, alcohol. The same "buzz" needs an increasing amount of alcohol. An adult who is addicted to gambling wants to play more to get the same high. They "chase" their losses in some cases, hoping they could win back lost money if they continue to engage in gambling. There are a vicious circle and an increased desire for activity. The strength to avoid decreases at the same time. The ability to control the urge to play is weakened as the craving increases in intensity and frequency.

This can have a professional, political, physical, social, or psychological impact. Neither the gambling frequency nor the amount lost will decide whether gambling is an individual problem. Many people engage rather than frequently in daily gambling binges, but the emotional and financial consequences will be the same. Gambling becomes an issue whenever the individual is no longer able to stop doing it and causes a negative effect on any area of the life of the individual.

Statistical Proof Estimates of the number of people who play socially and qualify for a gambling addiction diagnosis vary from 2% to 3%, impacting millions of people in the USA alone. Other important statistics on problem gambling include that it tends to have an international impact on at least 1 percent of people. In fact, teenagers tend to suffer from this condition twice as much as adults.

Although it is thought that more men than women suffer from pathological gambling, women are developing this disorder at higher rates, now accounting for as much as 25 percent of pathological gambling individuals. Other statistics about compulsive gambling are that during their early teenage years, men tend to develop this disorder, while women tend to develop it later. Then, though, women's disorder tends to get worse at a much faster rate than men. Many seemingly gender-based gambling addiction disparities include men's tendency to be addicted to more relational types of gaming, such as blackjack, craps, or poker, while women tend to participate in less interpersonal betting, such as slot machines or bingo. Men with pathological gambling tend to receive advice less often than their female counterparts on issues other than gambling.

Problem gambling generally involves gambling involving more than one symptom but less than the five or more symptoms required to qualify for compulsive or pathological gambling diagnosis. Binge gambling is a subtype of compulsive gambling that involves gambling problems, but only for certain periods of time. This is different from a general addiction to gambling, which appears to include excessive gambling activity regularly and to include recurrent thoughts (concern) about gambling, even when the individual is not involved in gambling.

Scientific and biological research on obsessive-compulsive factors and pathological gambling in an Italian study Gambling activity tends to be repetitive and difficult to avoid and seems to be directed at neutralizing or minimizing negative feelings such as anxiety and stress, indicating its similarities to the obsessive-compulsive continuum.

Based on gambling habits and obsessive-compulsive attitudes, a study of 300 Italian subjects was evaluated. The test took place in small centers in Italy, primarily in coffee and cigarette shops where slot machines are situated, using the South Oaks Gambling Screen (SOGS) and the MOCQ-R, a shortened version of Maudsley Obsessional-Compulsive Questionnaire.

A negative association between SOGS and MOPQ-R was observed in most of the subjects tested with respect to the control and cleaning subscales. Both instruments that evaluated demonstrated reliability and a strong capacity for discriminative purposes.

The study showed that the group of gamblers we studied did not belong to the field of obsessive-compulsive disorders, confirming the validity of the DSM-5 model for PG classification. Similar findings reflect the value of engaging in similar therapies to those used for conditions of drug use.

4.1 Pathological gambling

It is defined as a maladaptive and reoccurring pattern of gambling behaviors that persists despite significant negative effects on individuals, their work, and their families. This destructive conduct is often associated with increased psychological, legal, and financial issues. The prevalence of this social activity in Italy is rising as it has been estimated that at least once in a year, 54 percent of the Italian adult population (between the ages of 18 and 74) is gambling. There are nearly 30 million gamblers divided into different categories of sports, and in four years, the use of money for gaming, betting, and raffling has risen from € 6,000 million to € 17,000 million.

For teenagers, PG has also been identified, presenting important prevention issues. DSM-5 currently includes PG in the category of addictive disorders: it is referred to as a gambling disorder (GD) and is the only new addiction included, being the only one "without a drug." GD has many parallels with substance use disorders (SUDs), such as gradual loss of control over behavior, desire for euphoric or "strong" state, addiction, resistance, and symptoms of withdrawal. Often identified were the biological bases of PG, which is one of the reasons for its inclusion in the DSM-5 addiction portion.

PG also has many parallels to obsessive-compulsive disorder (OCD), but no less significant. Nevertheless, until the new manual was written, the discussion on how to classify PG, whether as an addictive disorder or as an obsessive-compulsive spectrum disorder, remained open.

Some scholars developed the idea of obsessive-compulsive related disorders in the early 1990s and applied to a class of conditions that share similarities with OCD. OCD is the compulsive disorder form. Obsessions are defined as recurring and persistent thoughts, perceived as intrusive by the subject. Compulsive behaviors are defined as goal-directed action that is repetitive, rigid, and stereotyped; individuals refer to being driven to perform them to avoid or reduce perceived negative effects. The gambling problem described in the DSM-5 resembles the obsessive thoughts usually found in patients suffering from OCD; in addition, the gambling activity tends to be repetitive and difficult to avoid and seems to be directed at neutralizing or minimizing negative moods such as anxiety and stress, again indicating parallels with OCD.

It was proposed that addiction compulsiveness arises from a dysregulation of particular neurochemical elements involved in brain reward and stress systems. The allostatic mechanism between reward function loss and brain stress system replacement provides a powerful basis for the creation of negative states that lead to compulsive behaviors (negative reward).

One theory suggests including the anhedonia factor of compulsive behavior. The loss of hedonic ability, possibly resulting in an underlying neuropsychological disorder, may be crucial in deciding the participation in regular and prolonged episodes of gambling, which, given negative consequences, reflect a compensatory effort to counterbalance tonic anhedonia. This theory was also suggested for other forms of addiction.

From different perspectives, the relationship between gambling disorder and obsessive-compulsive disorder was studied. Most research has to do with the phenomenological aspects of these two disorders.

Several pieces of researches also compared PG and OCD from the viewpoint of personality, finding differences in the dimensions of personality, and pointing out that patients with PG and OCD share similar profiles.

In 1999, Blaszczynski evaluated the presence of obsessions and compulsions in PG subjects using the Padua Inventory and highlighted specific outcomes of obsessiveness in pathological gamblers compared to subjects of control. On the other hand, the results were not confirmed by Won Kim and Grant's study, and other studies reported that PG shares more similarities with SUDs than OCD. Further research has also shown that other dimensions, such as the search for novelty and self-transcendence, are present. In addition, in an attempt to integrate knowledge in the field of pathological gambling, a 2008 review proposed a new theoretical model of three specific PG subtypes, which could be useful in finding more suitable treatments for the different subtypes. The obsessive-compulsive subtype is one of the three, different from the addictive subtype and the impulsive subtype. The authors pointed out that the OC subtype involves around 20-25% of players, mainly women, who establish gambling behaviors in reaction to negative psychological conditions, indicating that this group may respond better to antidepressants, SSRIs, and psychotherapy-related SNRIs.

A more new study, performed on an Italian sample, evaluated the prevalence of players of the different subtypes, showing a strong but not predominant presence of the OC subtype in the sample population; researchers also considered a possible combination of the different subtypes, indicating the effectiveness of different treatments for each of them. Differentiating into subtypes, as previously described in other research, is probably the right way to assess drug dependencies.

4.2 Gambling Addiction Signs and Symptoms

Gambling addiction is a form of the impulse-control disorder where you have little or no control over your gambling compulsion, even if you are conscious that your actions will harm you and others and even if the odds are against you.

There is often an underlying issue that causes you to continue playing games. Examples may include stress caused by work-related problems, unresolved relationship issues, drug or alcohol abuse, or a type of bereavement escapism, or any difficult emotional time in your life.

At first, we understand that it can be difficult at first to recognize that you have a gambling problem and to seek help. Whether you've lost a significant amount of money on one bet or over a period of time, your addiction to gambling can be corrected regardless of how severe your habit is.

Feeling a relentless urge to play even in a difficult financial state, or gambling as a way out of financial problems are both common symptoms of gambling addiction. Gambling addiction may also cause problems in relationships and at work, while the cost of financing a gambling addiction can become both an enormous burden and emotional pressure.

Excessive gambling emotional symptoms also trigger a variety of emotional symptoms, including anxiety, depression, and even suicidal thoughts and impulses. Such feelings can lead a gambler in extreme situations to actually make an attempt to end their lives. Losing all to gambling is devastating and leaves a lot of people feeling helpless.

Since gambling can cause depression, anxiety, and self-harming behavior, there are several physical signs of being identified. Depression and anxiety often contribute to lack of sleep, which under the eyes can lead to skin getting pale, weight gain or weight loss, acne, and dark circles.

4.3 Causes and Risk Factors for Gambling Addiction

It is vital to understand that there is generally no specific cause for pathological gambling when considering why people are playing. Several potential examples include the finding that in order to develop impulse-control disorders such as compulsive gambling, shopping, or compulsive sexual behaviors, several individuals given drugs to cure Parkinson's disease or restless leg syndrome were observed. The explanation of this relation includes the increased activity in the brain of the chemical messenger dopamine. One example that compulsive gambling may have a single cause is bipolar disorder because of exorbitant expenditure, including compulsive gambling, maybe a mania symptom that is part of bipolar disorder.

Much more generally, gambling addiction is described as the result of a combination of biological factors, ways of thinking, and social stressors (bio-psychosocial model), like most other emotional disorders. Nevertheless, there are elements that make the person more likely to develop a gambling addiction. Schizophrenia, mood problems, antisocial, alcohol and personality disorder, or drug use are risk factors for the development of pathological gambling. Individuals with low serotonin levels in the brain are also thought to be at higher risk compared to others for developing pathological gambling.

People who are suffering from compulsive gambling tend to be seekers of excitement, feel disconnected (dissociated), happy, or excited while playing video games or playing. Research also shows that individuals with money problems early in gambling earn a large amount of money, suffer a recent loss (such as divorce, job loss), or are lonely increases the risk of compulsive gambling. Easy access to gambling (e.g., living near towns with plenty of gambling resources, such as Las Vegas or Atlantic City), believing that they have discovered a winning gambling system and attempting to keep a record of money won and lost gambling are much more risk factors for compulsive gambling.

Causes as Cataloged by the DSM-5

the development of gambling disorder may begin in

puberty or young adulthood, but it occurs in middle or even older adulthood in other individuals. Gambling behavior usually progresses over the years, although in females, the development tends to be quicker than in males. Many people who develop a gambling problem display a gambling trend that gradually increases both in frequency and wagering numbers Milder types will, of course, grow into more serious cases.

Many people with gambling disorder claim that one or two types of gambling are most troublesome for them, even though some people are involved in many forms of gambling. Individuals are likely to engage more often in certain forms of gambling (buying daily scratch tickets) than others (playing weekly casino slot machines or blackjack). Gambling frequency can be more related to the type of gambling than to the nature of the gambling condition as a whole. Buying a single scratch ticket every day, for example, may not be troublesome, while less regular casinos, sporting, or card gaming may be part of a gambling condition. Likewise, in terms of gambling behavior, amounts of money spent on wagering are not in themselves. Some people may wager thousands of dollars a month and have no gambling problem, while others may wager much smaller amounts but experience significant gambling-related difficulties.

Gambling trends may be frequent or episodic, and the disorder of gambling may be persistent or in relapse. During periods of stress or depression, and in periods of use or abstinence, gambling can increase. There may be extreme gambling periods and serious issues, times of complete abstinence, and un-problematic gambling periods. Spontaneous, long-term remissions are sometimes associated with gambling illness. However, some people underestimate their susceptibility to developing a gambling disorder or returning to a gambling disorder after remission.

Early gambling disorder presentation is more prevalent among males than for females. People who start playing games with youth often do so with family members or friends. Early-life gambling disorder progression seems to be associated with impulsiveness and misuse of drugs. Most high school and college students who develop gambling disorder over time mature out of condition, although for some, it remains a lifelong problem, the onset of gambling disorder in mid-and later-life is more common among women than among men.

The type of gambling behaviors and the incidence levels of gambling illness differ in age and gender. In younger and middle-aged people, gambling disorder is more common than in older adults. The disease is more common in males than females among adolescents and young adults. Younger people prefer different forms of gambling (sports betting), whereas older adults are more likely to develop slot machines and bingo gambling problems. While the proportion of individuals seeking gambling disorder care is small across all age groups, it is particularly unlikely that younger individuals will seek treatment.

Males are more likely to start gambling early in life and have a younger age than females who are more likely to start gambling later in life and acquire gambling disorder in a shorter period of time. Females with gambling disorders are likely to face depressive, bipolar, and anxiety disorders than males with gambling disorders. Females also have a later age at the onset of the disorder and seek treatment earlier, despite low rates of seeking treatment among people with gambling disorder regardless of gender.

Common signs of gambling addiction may be triggered by underlying stress associated with a stressful time in your life, whether a job, relationship or financially related, as well as having an addictive personality prone to compulsive behavior.

There are also underlying emotional reasons that can contribute to the development and vicious cycle of compulsive gambling, including

- Overcoming social isolation by visiting betting shops or casinos

- Feeling a rush of adrenaline and dopamine as a' good' release of chemical brain

- Numb, uncomfortable emotions and issues that cannot be solved easily

- Boredom and a desire to spend time

- Losing a companion as a result of gambling addiction is quite common due to the pressures and stresses that the issue of gambling imposes on a partnership

- Workplace issues that could include an increased workload, lack of work or a general lack of concentration that makes it hard to complete tasks sufficiently

- Dissimulating the amount of money and time spent on family betting the stigma that is often involved with gambling problems leads to a lack of confidence and often more problems at home

Denial that you have a gambling problem is a big concern as the first step to rehabilitation is to acknowledge that you have a problem.

- Problem with gambling and loss of interest in other aspects of life, such as avoiding family responsibilities and focusing solely on gambling outcomes Pathological gambling includes chronic and recurring gambling problems that include several of the symptoms listed that are not the result of another mental health problem, such as during a manic episode:

4.4 Triggers

Gambling can lead to a range of issues, but it can happen to anyone with an addiction. No one can tell who is going to develop a gambling addiction.

Gambling conduct becomes a problem when it cannot be regulated and interferes with jobs, relationships, and the workplace. The person may not know for some time that they have a problem.

Many people who create a gambling addiction are considered responsible and reliable individuals, but some factors may lead to behavioral change.

These may include:

- Retirement
- Stressful situations

Work-related stress

- Emotional upheavals, such as depression or anxiety
- Isolation
- Existence of other addictions

Environmental factors,

Such as friends or opportunities available, Studies have suggested that people with a propensity to develop another habit. A role may be played by genetic and neurological factors.

Many people affected by gambling may also have an alcohol or drug problem, possibly due to an addiction predisposition.

Some alcohol use was associated with a higher risk of compulsive gambling.

Secondary addictions may also arise in an attempt to reduce the negative feelings generated by addiction to gambling. Most people who play never encounter any other addiction, however.

There are a few factors

These include:

- Depression, anxiety or personality disorders
- Certain addictions, such as drugs or alcohol
- The use of other medications, such as antipsychotic medicines and dopamine agonists, related to a higher risk of gambling addiction
- Sex, it is more likely to affect men than women. Need to play for excitement

2 with growing amounts of money. Restlessness or irritability while attempting to stop playing

3. Repeated attempts to stop, regulate, or raising gambling

4 have been ineffective. Always thinking about playing games and making plans to play 5. Gambling 6 when you feel depressed. Going back to gambling after losing money

7. Lying to hide the activities of gambling

8. Because of gambling 9, having a relationship, or work problems. Depending on others for cash to spend on gambling

An overview of signs and symptoms take a deeper look at some of the symptoms described above: You can't stop those who are playing for fun limit themselves and their bets. Compulsive gamblers are struggling with both their spending time and money. Betting takes over their lives, and they are continually wagering. They're trying to quit, but they can't.

You're playing with money that you can't afford to lose problem gamblers don't end with "fun money" being set aside for betting. They use the money spent on taxes, insurance, or education for their children. They not only squandered their last penny at times but also borrowed money.

The interviewed psychologist Stacy said one of his patients had borrowed such unsavory money from sources that he would put the safety of his family at risk.

Your bets go beyond casual gamblers playing for fun and spending a couple of dollars to have a good time. For reasons other than enjoyment, gambling addicts place bets, often attempting to escape depression or other problems. Whatever problems you face, it's not the solution to gambling.

You try to recover losses by playing more. Have you tried repeatedly to get back the money by betting more that you lost gambling? Problem gamblers will see more betting as a financial loss solution than it is-throwing money at the problem.

You are playing with ever more money like other addictions; small pathological gambling may begin. Yet problem gamblers are not going to be happy to keep the stakes small or set limits. To feel the rush, they need to bet more and more.

Pathological gamblers don't quit gambling when their bank account runs dry; you go to lengths to find money to play. Instead, to find more money, they go to extremes. While this may stop borrowing, some problem gamblers use fraud, falsification, or other crimes to fuel their habit.

Before more important matters, you put gambling problem gamblers to allow their habit to prioritize other parts of their lives. A gambling addict may skip watching the soccer game of her child or missing time to hit the casino at work. Careers are thrown on the back burner, and relationships fail at the cost of their habit.

Gambling has a negative effect on your emotions. Though gambling can be an exciting experience, addicts can experience emotions that signify a problem, including:

• Frustration or disappointment when you've tried to quit and struggle

• Remorse feelings

• A decline in motivation

• The desire to celebrate an unexpected gambling occurrence. If you think you're addicted, there are steps to help you quit. The key to saving your career, relationships, and bank account is to take early action.

Complications and Negative impacts of Gambling Addiction Although as many as one-third of people suffering from pathological gambling can recover from the disease without any treatment, the potential damage that compulsive gambling can cause in the life of the patient and those around it clearly indicates that the potential positive implications outweigh the potential complications. Each year in the United States, as much as $5 billion is spent on gambling, with people who are addicted to gambling accumulating tens of thousands of dollars in debt. Bad effects that compulsive gambling can have on the victim include financial problems ranging from high debt, bankruptcy, or deprivation, to legal problems arising from fraud to prostitution, lust, attempt, or suicide completion. Most compulsive gambling sufferers experience medical problems associated with stress, such as insomnia, stomach ulcers, and other gastrointestinal problems, headaches, and muscle aches. Gambling addiction can have a variety of adverse family effects. Statistics show that families with compulsive gambling individuals are more likely to experience domestic violence and abuse of children. Kids of problem gamblers are at significantly higher risk of depression, behavioral problems, and misuse of drugs. One of the drawbacks of compulsive gambling care is that as many as two-thirds of people starting treatment for this condition delay premature treatment, whether it includes medication, counseling, or both.

A manic episode does not describe gambling activity better.

Gambling addiction affects 1 to 3 % of all-age people, men more often than women. It usually starts in men and later in women in puberty. Although casino and sports betting are limited to just a few states, there has been a proliferation of other gaming venues, including riverboat and Indian casinos, state and national lotteries, and Internet access to offshore sports and parlor betting. The connection has dramatically increased. Older adults are often more vulnerable to gambling losses than other age groups due to their reliance on fixed incomes and reduced ability to recover.

Those with pathological behavior in gambling often have alcohol and other drugs, depression, and anxiety issues. Individuals with pathological behavior in gambling also take suicide into account.

Individuals with pathological gambling behavior, including bankruptcy, divorce, job loss, and prison time, appear to have personal, social, and legal issues. Gambling stress can also lead to heart attacks in at-risk individuals. The right treatment can help to avoid many of these issues.

4.5 Gambling Addiction Facts and Effects

- Compulsive gambling affects 2%-3% of Americans can involve a variety of ways and places to bet, and symptoms may differ slightly between males and females, as well as between adults and adolescents.

- While men tend to develop gambling addiction at a higher rate and younger than women, women now make more than one-quarter of all compulsive gamblers, and women's symptoms appear to escalate more quickly once compulsive gambling develops.

- The problem of gambling involves more than one but less than five symptoms of compulsive gambling as opposed to pathological gambling.

- Although the direct causes of compulsive gambling are unusual, the development of this disorder has been associated with manic episodes associated with bipolar disorder and certain medications that treat Parkinson's disease and restless leg syndrome.

Schizophrenia, mood problems, antisocial personality disorder, alcohol, or cocaine addiction are risk factors for pathological gambling.

- Diagnosis of compulsive gambling includes recognizing at least five signs suggesting impaired gambling impulse control and excluding any potential causes of behavior.

- Like any mental health condition, a successful diagnosis of gambling addiction requires a complete physical and psychological assessment, including a mental-state evaluation and sufficient laboratory tests to rule out other possible causes of the symptoms being observed.

- Compulsive gambling care typically uses more than one method, including psychotherapy, medications, financial counseling, support groups, 12-step programs, and self-help.

- Therapy is positive for the prognosis of recovery from compulsive gambling.

- While pathological gambling can be overcome in many individuals on its own, the devastating consequences it typically has on the social, family, legal and mental health status of the person suggest that therapy must be managed by anyone who is encouraged to seek assistance for this condition.

- Compulsive gambling treatment generally involves mitigating risk factors and educate the public on the warning signs of this condition.

Short-Term and Long-Term Effects of a Gambling Addiction

Gambling is associated with many more short-and long-term effects. Addiction to gambling also leads to other addictions that serve as coping mechanisms for people overwhelmed by the practice. Most gamblers turn to drugs, alcohol, and other behaviors to relieve the anxiety caused by the lifestyle of gambling. Even if a gambler never suffers financial ruin as a result of lifestyle, after self-medicating to deal with stress, they can struggle with drug and alcohol addiction for the rest of life. Often, as a result of gambling, relationships are often permanently damaged.

Check or Self-Assessment for Gambling Addiction When you think you're having a gambling problem, ask yourself if you'd be all right now if you'd stopped playing. If you're nervous or you're not supposed to stop yet, you're likely to suffer from a gambling addiction. If you're not sure, though, call our hotline to talk to someone who can help you determine if you have a problem and need assistance in recovery.

CHAPTER 5: Effects on Family and Relationships

5.1 Effects of Problem Gambling on Families

Intimate partners and other family members, including children, parents, siblings, and grandparents, are affected by gambling problems. Gambling issues affect family life and close relationships.

Impaired family relationships, emotional issues, and financial difficulties are some of the most common impacts of gambling problems on family members.

There is consistent evidence that gambling issues are associated with family violence.

The kids of problem gambling parents are at a much higher risk of developing gambling issues than the kids of non-problem parents.

The effects of gambling issues on intimate relationships were divided into three distinct phases:

(1) The denial phase,

(2) The stress phase, and

(3) The exhaustion phase (Custer & Milt, 1985).

Recent research indicates that people with gambling problems have intimate relationships involving poor communication, relationship and sexual dissatisfaction, conflict and disagreements, and the possibility of separation or divorce (Dowling, Smith, & Thomas, 2009; Hodgins, Shead, & Makarchuk, 2007).

Increased gambling Questions unpaid bills Depression Phase Spouse spends less time with the family Arguments Spouse feels rejected Attempts to control gambling Exhaustion Phase Learning impaired Confusion Physical symptoms Immobilization Anger Anxiety and fear impact on children when they feel rejected Many kids may be neglected, discouraged, and frustrated. They might assume that they caused the problem and that the problem would stop if they are "healthy." Many kids are looking after younger brothers or sisters or trying to support their parents. Kids are overwhelmed by this obligation.

Kids may also feel that their parents have to take sides. We may cease to trust a parent who promises not to keep him or her. At school, they can steal from the parent or get into trouble. Many young people may attempt to draw attention away from the parent with the issue of gambling by• Using alcohol or other drugs • Gambling• Breaking the law. It is important to help children understand that their fault is not the problem of the family. It is important for children to return to a healthy and happy home life and a normal childhood. Family or individual counseling may help kids navigate these shifts.

Problem gambling and recent suicide research have shown a strong connection between gambling issues and suicidal thoughts–more than twice the number of people affected by gambling issues claim they consider taking their own lives compared to those not affected by gambling.

There is a limit to how much a person's body can take before they need medical intervention with other addictions, such as drugs or alcohol. Gambling isn't like that, and often for a long time, a downward spiral can go unchecked. Especially if there are large amounts of debt involved, there may seem to be no other option.

If you are self-harmed or have suicidal thoughts or feelings, it is important to seek professional assistance as soon as possible.

5.2 Impacts on Family Environments

Beyond intimate partners.

The family atmosphere of people with gambling problems is also marked by high levels of anger and confrontation as well as low levels of clear and effective contact, less freedom, less engagement in intellectual and cultural activities, lack of commitment and encouragement, little direct expression of feelings and less participation in social activities (Ciarrocchi & Such social dynamics are equivalent to drinking-problem people (Ciarrocchi & Hohmann, 1989). In addition, gambling-related children are exposed to a variety of family stressors, including financial and emotional deprivation, physical isolation, inconsistent supervision, parental neglect/abuse and rejection, inadequate role-modeling, family conflict, and diminished security and stability (Darbyshire, Oster, & Carrig, 2001).

Common Family Members Problems Common gambling issues reported by family members include:

- Loss of household or personal money
- Arguments
- Anger and violence
- Lies and deception
- Family neglect
- Neglected relationships
- Poor communication

- Confusion of family roles and responsibilities

- Development of family gambling problems or other addictions

- Many people.

- Friendships may end due to unpaid debts Relationship between Gambling Problems and Domestic violence There is now consistent global evidence that gambling issues are more closely linked to intimate partner violence (IPV) and domestic violence (Dowling et al., in press). Relationships are complex; however, people with gambling issues are more likely to be victims and perpetrators of IPV than people without gambling issues.

The World Health Organization (2002) describes IPV as any activity that causes physical, psychological, or sexual damage to those in that relationship within an intimate relationship. This may include physical abuse, sexual abuse, mental (psychological) abuse, and behavior management. As per a systematic review of globally available research (Dowling et al., in the press), more than one-third of individuals with gambling troubles report being victims of physical IPV (38%) or IPV (37%) perpetrators. In fact, 11% of IPV victims report gambling issues.

While most evidence relates to intimate relationships, there is some evidence that victimization and violence perpetration leads to children and other members of the wider family (Dowling, Jackson, et al., 2014; Dowling et al., in the press; Suomi et al., 2013). Over half of people to gambling problems (56%) report physical violence against their kids (Dowling et al., in press), according to the systematic review. In addition, several recent Australian studies have found that between one-third and one-half (34-53%) of people with gambling problems and family members experience any form of family abuse In the previous 12 months (victimization (27-41%), perpetration (23-33%); Dowling, Jackson, et al., 2014; Suomi et al., 2013). In these studies, the most common perpetrators and victims of family violence were parents, current partners, and former partners. Nevertheless, it is important to view with care the results of studies involving family members other than spouses. Only a few studies of recorded prevalence estimates are available with significant variability. Furthermore, many studies are not representative of the general population, include only a small number of problem gamblers, use categories that may encounter multiple problems in addition to issues related to gambling, and use different definitions of abuse. More research is needed to remind the family of the association between problem gambling and crime.

5.3 Effects on the Health and Wellbeing of Family Members

Intimate partners and children are adversely affected by gambling problems in various ways (Dickson-Swift, James & Kippen, 2005; Hodgins, Shead, et al., 2007; Vitaro, Wanner, Brendgen & Tremblay, 2008). There are common mental issues, physical ailments, and behavioral problems.

Emotional Disturbances of Intimate Partners Rage Resentment Depression Anxiety Emotional Disturbances of Children Depression Anxiety Confusion Guilt Physical Problems of Intimate Partners Symptoms Gastrointestinal Disturbances Hypertension Physical Issues of Children Asthma Allergies Chronic symptoms Psychological Disturbances of Intimate Partners By taking on more tasks, one member can try to keep things under check. This may result in burnout. Family members frequently concentrate on the gambling problem individual and forget about taking care of themselves or having fun.

Passing Problem Gambling from one generation to the next the children of trouble gambling parents are also at risk of developing their own gambling problems. Findings from four independent studies investigating the intergenerational and family transmission of gambling issues found that people with a gambling problem having a parent or sibling is two to ten times more likely to experience gambling issues than people without a parent or sibling with a gambling problem. Individuals with gambling problem fathers were 11 to 14 times more likely to have gambling problems, and people with gambling problem mothers were 7 to 11 times more likely to have gambling problems.

Risk factors

- Gambling at a young age

- Parental drug and mental health problems

- Personal drug use

- Gambling to reduce negative emotions or increase positive emotions • Gambling for socialize

- Expecting gambling will lead to positive outcomes (e.g., feelings of control or financial gain) Protective factors

- Being female

- Having increased social resources and networks
- To have more siblings
- Expecting gambling will lead to negative outcomes (e.g., depression or over-involvement

Financial Impact on the Gambler

There is a reason why people consider problem gambling addiction–it can be really hard to stop, close to a chemical addiction to nicotine or another drug in some ways. This is because when gamblers win, dopamine, a chemical in our brain that makes us feel happy, appears to be released. This chemical reaction in the brain is one of the factors contributing to addiction feelings, and other brain-related factors may also be involved. Dr. Franco Manes, a neurological researcher, suggests that impairments in the pre-frontal cortex of the brain may make it harder for a problem gambler to consider future consequences accurately. Impulse management and decision-making by executives can also be impaired. Both biological and neurological factors can strongly tax an individual's gambling problem, causing severe stress, anxiety, or feelings of helplessness. Financial repercussions can also pile up, as Problem Gambling records these individuals losing around $21,000 a year–

that's one-third of a nationwide average income. Because of the addictive chemical causes of gambling, it can be very difficult for a problem gambler to leave. Financial Effect on Family Members another AGRC study found that financial pressures, disrupted relationships, lack of trust, and other emotionally upsetting effects were the three most common negative effects of extreme gambling on families. The most common issue is money loss. You can suddenly lose your money, properties, or belongings. Such a money crisis makes the family feel afraid, furious and betrayed. A build-up of these negative emotions may cause relationships to break down. In reality, Problem Gambling focused on problem gamblers in a study on depression and relationship issues, finding that they are six times more likely to divorce, four times more likely to have problems with alcohol, and four times more likely to smoke regularly. One research by The Problem Gambling Treatment and Research Center showed that problem gambler children are ten times more likely to follow their parents ' footsteps once they become adults. The AGRC stresses that these conditions can leave family members and loved ones with adverse effects on their own health, particularly if their attempts to dissuade or change the gambling behavior of the problem fail. Such cases may benefit more from professional assistance so that all sides are considered equally, and the opinions of all are respected and treated carefully

Chapter 6: How can Family Rescue Problem Gambler and Control Finances

How to Help Loved One from Gambling If you have a gambling problem with your loved one, you probably have a lot of feelings that clash. You may have spent a lot of time and money trying to avoid cheating or having to cover your loved one for them. At the same time, you may be angry about your loved one again for playing games and sick of trying to keep up the charade. Your loved one may have borrowed or stolen money without any way of repaying it. They may have sold family property or worked on joint credit cards with huge debts.

Although compulsive and depressed gamblers need their family and friends ' support to help, they avoid gambling in their struggle, their decision to quit must be theirs. You can't make someone quit gambling as much as you want, and as hard as it sees the results. You should, however, empower them to seek help, assist them in their efforts, protect themselves, and take seriously any talk of suicide.

Preventing suicide in problem gamblers if a problem gambler faces the consequences of his actions, he can suffer a crippling decrease in self-esteem. This is one reason why compulsive gamblers have a high suicide rate.

Problem gamblers are much more likely to attempt suicide, according to a landmark report that sparked government calls to do more to counter the risks of gambling.

Studies conducted by Gamble Aware, a major UK gaming organization, found that problem gamblers were six times more likely to have suicidal thoughts or threaten to take their own lives–and might be 15 times more likely to do so.

Even when accounting for other contributing factors that could be related to suicidal thoughts such as depression, substance abuse, and financial problems, the elevated risk persisted.

The researchers found that excluding these causes, problem gamblers were still three times more likely to consider or attempt suicide.

Nearly one out of five, or 19 percent, had considered suicide in the past year compared to 4.1 percent of the general population, while 4.7 percent had attempted suicide compared to 0.6 percent in the broader population.

Dr. Heather, assistant professor at the London School of Hygiene and Tropical Medicine, co-author of the report, said the results of the study would cause swifter action to protect addicts, particularly within the industry.

"Gambling harms are significant and can be detrimental to persons, families, and communities; she said. These results show how people having gambling problems are a higher risk group for suicidality. "The people at the forefront of coping with this high-risk group are the industry, who need to think about how they prepare workers with encounters with suicidal people potentially. Charles and Liz Ritchie, who created the charity Gambling with Lives after their son Jack killed himself when he was addicted to gambling at the age of 24, said the study showed the need for greater government action.

The Ritchies want to hold the government legally liable for the death of their son, blaming the industry for lax regulation.

Identifying and addressing suicidal thoughts A family member may have thoughts of suicide if he or she:

- Changes in behavior, appearance or mood
- Seems depressed, sad or withdrawn
- Gives away precious possessions
- Talks about suicide and says that he or she has a plan
- Makes a will or talks about final wishes. If this happens, you should:
- Take all suicide threats seriously
- Stay calm and listen to care. Do not pass judgment or try to solve the issue
- Ask if the person feels suicidal and has a plan
- Remove all means of self-harm (e.g., weapons, medicines)
- Support the person in seeking professional assistance (e.g., crisis line, psychiatrist, doctor, emergency room or clergy)
- Keep your doctor be aware of what is going on
- Do not agree to keep the person's suicidal thoughts a secret
- Talk to someone who is willing to do so.

6.1 Tips for Family Members

Start by helping yourself

You have the right to emotionally and financially secure yourself. Do not blame yourself for the problems of the gambler or let your life be governed by his or her addiction. Ignoring your own needs may be a burnout formula.

Don't do it alone. It may be so difficult to deal with the gambling addiction of a loved one that it may seem easier to rationalize their desires "this last time." Or you may feel ashamed, feeling as if you are the only one that has issues like this. Reaching for help will make you realize that this dilemma has been faced by many families.

Set money management guidelines Consider taking over the family finances to ensure that the gambler remains responsible and to prevent a recurrence. This will not mean, however, that you are responsible for micromanaging the impulses of the problem gambler to play. Your first duty is to ensure that there is no danger to your own finances and credit.

Remember how demands for money are treated by problem gamblers often become very good to ask for money, either directly or indirectly. To obtain it, they may use begging, bribery, or even threats. It takes practice to ensure that you do not encourage the gambling addiction of your loved one.

Do's and Don'ts for Problem Gamblers Partners Do Talk to your partner if you're cool and not worried or upset about their problem gambling and its effects.

Look for support for families of problem gamblers such as self-help groups and reach out to people who have faced the same obstacles.

Explain to your partner that you are looking for help because you and your family are affected by their gambling.

Talk to your kids about the gambling issue of your parents.

Manage the family finances, track bank, and credit card statements carefully.

Encourage and support your loved one during the care of their problem of gambling, even if it may be a long process of setbacks.

Don't lose your temper, preach, teach, or make threats and ultimatums that you can't keep going.

Overlook the positive quality of your partner.

Prevent family life and events from affecting your partner.

Expect the recovery of your partner from the gambling problem to be smooth or quick. Even if their gambling ceases, there may be other underlying issues.

The bailout of debt or allow your partner to play in any way.

Hide or deny the problem of your partner to yourself or others.

Rationally Approaching the Loved One about gambling does not presume that gambling problems are a process through which the individual is likely to pass. When you believe that your spouse has gambling problems, it's important to help him because the implications can be major. These may involve a breakup of marriages, financial issues, criminal penalties, job loss, family violence, and mental health issues.

If you are worried and are upset by the gambling of your partner, you should:

- Choose a convenient time and place to talk.

- Make sure you have enough time and meet in a private space away from distractions and interruptions.
- It is also important to plan for gambling problems by providing information on support.
- You should talk to the loved one about his gambling issues in a calm and rational way.
- First, tell him and your friendship with him about some positive things.
- It's important to discuss what habits you've encountered, instead of concentrating on the individual as the issue.
- Remove comments that might suggest that you're judging.
- Use 'I' statements instead of 'you' statements, e.g. 'I'm concerned when I don't know when you're coming home or how much money you're going to spend' rather than 'You're frustrated when you're late and wasting all of our money.'
- Make recommendations instead of telling the person what to do, e.g., 'would you be comfortable seeing a gambling counselor?

- Ask the loved one for his viewpoint, thus validating his experience and emotions, e.g., "I understand that gambling is important to you."

- Give the person enough time to tell his story, as it will allow him to open up and trust you.

You should not:

Speak, question, or argue with the person about their gambling issues

- Try to control the individual by threatening, bribing, crying, or nagging

- Use shame in an effort to force the person can change

- Attack the person verbally or physically. If you think that any negative attitudes towards the person's gambling or gambling, in general, hinder your ability to help the person, you should suggest that the person talks to someone else.

Be ready for the full range of responses you might receive, from relaxation to frustration, while talking to the loved one. The loved one may deny, minimize, rationalize, or lie about his problems with gambling, or blame others. Be aware that he or she may feel embarrassed or ashamed and may not want to speak. You are using empathy and compassion to reduce the chances of this happening. If the person doesn't want to talk about gambling issues, you can tell him or her about available gambling help, and you're willing to talk when he or she's ready. If the conversation becomes unproductive or aggressive, the discussion should be stopped, and you should try again.

Encouraging medical assistance Effective professional assistance for gambling issues is available. Not everyone needs or wants professional assistance, though. Treatment targets may be to abstain from gambling or to set limits on gambling practices. Familiarize yourself with the effective treatments available for gambling issues and encourage the loved one to seek the most appropriate type of help. You must also familiarize yourself with the available local resources to help people with gambling issues, so you can tell him or her about these when you talk to the loved one. These services may include professional gambling services, resources for self-help, support groups, mechanisms for self-exclusion, and culturally diverse services.

Since financial issues can be a major part of gambling, you should be aware of tools that can help your loved one solve financial problems. The loved one might also need to access other types of gambling-related issues such as medical assistance, legal services, mental health care, financial advice, vocational rehab, or social assistance. In pointing out that:

- Gambling problems can be successfully treated, you can motivate him or her to seek professional help for gambling issues. Professional help, support groups, and self-help approaches have helped many individuals with gambling problems.

- It is a sensible thing to seek help for a problem, rather than a sign of weakness.

- The earlier the question is dealt with, the faster it can be resolved.

- All medical aid shall be confidential.

Encouraging the family member to improve It is not your personal responsibility to' fix' the gambling problems of the individual. You should persuade the member of the family to improve, though. Do not expect the gambling habit to be moral about him or her or to change it immediately. Consult with the member of the family to decide on appropriate habits, such as talking to a therapist, staying within negotiated spending limits. Be clear about what you're able to do to support the family member and what habits you're going to tolerate, although you can change these limits over time.

• Think about the techniques that gambling companies use to keep people gambling and maximize profits, for example. Gaming machines are designed in a way to keep people playing and spending money

• Avoid going to gambling sites, even if they don't plan on gambling, for example, going to a pub for food where gambling is possible. These might include:

• Searching for encouragement from other family members, friends or others to help him reduce his gambling

• Eviting spending time with people associated with gambling habits

• Identifying and using ways to handle gambling impulses

• Setting and adhering to a budget

• If the family member is gambling online, using software programs that block or limit access

- Recognition

If this or any other self-help approaches are determined by the family member, offer to support him. Notice and congratulate him on any positive changes the person has made. It is important to focus on the future rather than past mistakes as the individual attempts to change his gambling. The person who stopped or reduced his gambling may notice a void in his life that was filled with gambling, e.g., reduction in social activities.

If that's the case, you can recommend things you can do with the person who doesn't include gambling (e.g., going to the movies or a restaurant) and reconnects with family and friends. Such social support can also relieve causes that can aggravate gambling issues like anxiety, frustration, stress, depression, or boredom.

6.2 Looking After your Finances

Money could be a sensitive subject for many people, and when there is a gambling problem, it can become even more sensitive. If you have a gambling problem with someone near you, you may need to secure your finances. These tips will help people and their circumstances for partners, family, and friends. Sometimes, when determining how to handle money issues, it's a good idea to talk to a financial advisor.

Protecting your Finances Family members are facing financial pressures from people with gambling problems. You may need to take on the role of looking after the finances of your family and managing access to money for your partner.

Together with a financial advisor, you might consider:

Having a family budget-try to make it realistic, especially when it comes to repaying debts so that the individual with a gambling problem does not feel the need for more gambling

- Careful monitoring of all family spending
- Managing family finances until the gambling is under control
- Agree on how much cash or loan your spouse has to pay.
- Thinking carefully about your own assets before offering financial assistance
- Paying bills yourself rather than lending money to bills

- Not sharing your PIN numbers

- Keeping your valuables and cash out of sight

- Warning your relatives, friends, and colleagues not to lend money to the individual

- Changing your will to ensure your potential wealth is not lost to gambling.

Strategies for Financial Management and Damage Control Lock your credit while "locking" a mutual credit account can temporarily prevent you from accessing your own funds, it will help prevent the situation from getting worse than it already has.

Open in your name only a new credit card and bank account

There are plenty of married couples who manage their finances completely separately. By removing your name from compromised accounts and creating new accounts that will only be open to you, you will prevent your loved ones from draining your funds while also ensuring that your credit score is safe.

Secure or move any of your long-term investments Gambling addicts are more likely to focus on long-term assets–college savings, retirement funds, holiday savings–as they will not have to deal with the consequences of these acts until much further down the road.

6.3 Speak with a financial advisor

In past situations similar to yours, professional financial advisors have undoubtedly worked with people. We may have expert advice about other actions that you can take.

If you're someone who has a gambling problem financially linked to the family member, it is significant to make sure that they do not have access to the resources that will make their problem worse. Many of these actions may, in the future, if necessary, be functionally "undone." Meanwhile, prevention of damage must be a top priority.

The above measures will help to prevent the situation from worsening. However, if the issue of gambling has existed for years, then other claims are likely to have to be addressed retroactively.

Here are a few things you can do to help get your financial situation back in order: arranging all your debts and consolidating debt restructuring, if possible, will help make your debts more manageable.

If you can pay this back in time, you can eventually be able to lower your monthly interest rates.

You are refinancing debts that are not especially urgent.

The prospect of refinancing is certainly worth considering whenever you are faced with an unforeseen source of financial obligations.

Help restore your reputation with a zero-interest credit card. If you have a gambling problem, your credit may need to be fixed.

Even if you only use the card for something as basic as a gum pack every month, it will help to improve your creditworthiness by regularly meeting such financial obligations.

Check for other financial sources Personal loans, government assistance, and additional income sources (entering the workplace or taking up a second job) are just a few of the ways you can boost the monthly cash flow of your family. In fact, it can aid you in different situations of refinancing.

Many lenders and credit card companies want you to be a client. Even if the current financial situation is less than optimal, as long as you are able to handle your loans responsibly, certain choices are likely to be within your control.

Chapter 7: Beating Gambling Addiction through Self-management

Self-Help for Problem Gamblers

The most significant step to overcoming an addiction to gambling is to realize you have a problem. To own up to this requires tremendous strength and courage, particularly if you've lost a lot of money along the way and strained or broken relationships.

Do not despair, and do not try to go it alone. Many others were in your shoes, breaking the habit and restoring their lives. You can do that, too.

Learn how to alleviate unpleasant feelings in healthier ways Are you playing when you're lonely or bored, after a stressful day at work, or after an argument with your spouse?

Gambling can be a means of calming, unwinding, or socializing unpleasant emotions.

There are safer and more effective ways to manage your moods and alleviate boredom, such as running, spending time with non-playing friends, taking on new activities, or practicing relaxation techniques.

Strengthen your support network without help it's hard to fight an addiction, so reach out to friends and family. There are ways to make new friends without depending on visiting casinos or online gambling if your support network is small. Try to reach out to co-workers, join a sports team or book club, participate in an education class or volunteer for a good cause.

For example, entering a peer support group Gamblers Anonymous is a 12-step recovery program based on anonymous alcoholics. A vital part of the program is to find a sponsor, a convicted gambler who has the experience that remains free of gambling and can provide you with invaluable guidance and support.

Depression, stress, substance abuse, or anxiety can both cause gambling problems and get worse by compulsive gambling. Even if gambling is no longer part of your life, these issues will remain, so resolving them is necessary.

For many problem gamblers, it's not stopping gambling but the biggest challenge is remaining in recovery making a lifelong commitment to stay away from gambling. The Internet has made gambling much more available and hence more difficult to rehab users in order to avoid recurrence. Digital casinos and bookmakers are available to anyone with a smartphone or computer access all day, every day.

If you surround yourself with people to whom you are accountable, avoid enticing environments and websites, give up control of your finances (at least at first), and pursue alternative activities to replace gambling in your life, sustaining recovery from gambling addiction or problem gambling is still possible.

Make Healthier Choices. One way to stop gambling is to remove and replace the conditions required for gambling to take place in your life with healthier choices.

The four conditions needed to continue gambling are a decision.

You need to make the decision to play for gambling to happen.

If you have an urge: stop what you're doing and call someone, think about the consequences of your acts, tell yourself to stop thinking about gambling, and find something else to do right away.

Without capital, money gambling can't happen. Get rid of your credit cards, let someone else be responsible for your money, get the bank to make automatic payments for you, close online betting accounts, and keep a limited amount of cash on you.

Time: you can't play online if you don't have the time. You have to prepare for your leisure time.

Find other ways to fill the quiet moments during your day if you're gambling on your mobile.

Gambling is a game in which there is no chance to play without a game or operation to bet.

Do not put yourself in situations that are enticing,

tell gambling establishments that you often have a problem with gambling and ask them to restrict your admission. Disable gambling applications on your mobile and computer and block gambling sites.

Maintaining recovery from gambling addiction depends a lot on finding alternative behaviors to replace gambling.

Some examples include:

To engage in a fun activity, get a rush of an adrenaline sport or a competitive task, such as mountain biking, rock climbing, or go-kart racing To be more social, overcome shyness or loneliness with counseling, join a public speaking class, enter a social group, interact with family and friends, volunteer, find new friends to numb unpleasant feelings, do not worry about problems.

Deep breathing, meditation, and massage solve many anxiety problems.

Prevent depression by contacting a trusted family member, meeting a friend for coffee, or going to a Gamblers Anonymous meeting the urge to play may pass or become weak enough to resist as you wait.

Visualize what happens if you succumb to the temptation to play. Talk about how you'll feel after all your money's gone and you've disappointed yourself and your family again.

Distract yourself with another task, such as going to the gym, watching a movie, or doing a gambling cravings relief exercise.

When you can't resist the temptation for gambling, don't be too harsh on yourself or use it as an excuse to give up.

It's a tough process to conquer a gambling addiction. From time to time, you will slip; the important thing is to learn from your mistakes and continue to work towards recovery.

Gambling Addiction Treatment these strategies may include compulsive gambling treatment:

7.1 Therapy

It may be useful for behavioral therapy or cognitive behavioral therapy. Behavioral therapy requires regular exposure to your unlearned actions and teaches you strategies to reduce the gambling urge.

Cognitive-behavioral therapy focuses on recognizing and changing good, optimistic, dysfunctional, unreasonable, and negative attitudes. It may also be helpful for family therapy.

Medicines Antidepressants and mood stabilizers can help with problems that often go hand in hand with compulsive gambling — like depression, OCD, or ADHD.

In reducing gambling activity, some antidepressants may be effective. Medicines called narcotic antagonists can help combat compulsive gambling, which is useful in treating substance abuse.

7.2 Self-help groups

Many people find that talking to others with a problem with gambling can be a valuable part of treatment. Ask for advice on self-help groups such as Gamblers Anonymous and other support from your health care professional.

Compulsive gambling services may include an outpatient program, hospital program, or residential treatment plan, depending on your needs and resources. Your compulsive gambling treatment plan may include medication for substance abuse, depression, anxiety, or any other mental health condition.

Relapse prevention you can return to gambling even with treatment, particularly if you spend time in gambling environments with people who play or you are in gambling.

Tell your mental health professional or mentor right away to head off a relapse if you fear you're going to start gambling again.

It's never easy to overcome a gambling issue, and looking for professional treatment doesn't mean you're deficient in some way or can't handle your issues. Every gambler is special, so you need a recovery program specifically tailored to your needs and circumstance.

Tell your doctor or mental health professional about different treatment options, including hospital or residential treatment, and rehabilitation programs are aimed at people with a serious gambling addiction who cannot stop gambling without round-the-clock assistance.

Treatment for underlying conditions that lead to your compulsive gambling, like misuse of drugs or mental health issues including depression, anxiety, OCD, or ADHD This may include changes in therapy, medicine, and lifestyle. Problem gambling will sometimes be a symptom of bipolar disorder, so before making a diagnosis, the doctor or therapist may have to rule out this.

CBT cognitive-behavioral therapy for gambling addiction focuses on modifying the habits and perceptions of pathological gambling, like rationalizations and false beliefs. It may also teach you how to fight the impulses of gambling and solve health, job, and relationship issues caused by gambling problems. Therapy will give you the tools to cope with your life-long addiction.

Family therapy and marriage, career counseling, and credit counseling will help you work through the specific issues generated by your gambling problem and lay the foundation for fixing your relationships and finances.

Problem and Pathological Gamblers Interventions:

Pharmacotherapies Small to moderate, randomized, short-term, placebo-controlled, and, with the exception of one research, flexible-dose clinical trials have been performed over the past several years to examine the efficacy and tolerability of different pharmacotherapies in the treatment of pathological gambling.

Two selective serotonin reuptake inhibitors (SSRIs; fluvoxamine and paroxetine), a µ-opioid blocker (naltrexone), and a mood stabilizer (lithium) have been shown to be superior to placebo in the treatment of patients with pathological gambling in the short term.

Of these, SSRIs and naltrexone research excluded people with significant co-occurring mental health/substance use disorders (excluding nicotine dependence), and progress in gambling symptomatology and overall clinical status was found in the absence of significant changes in mood and anxiety measurements.

A lithium study only included bipolar spectrum participants with pathological gambling, excluding psychotic disorders, and progress in gambling, mania, and general clinical status indicators were observed. A placebo-controlled trial of the atypical antipsychotic drug olanzapine in the treatment of video poker pathological gamblers found no increased effectiveness over placebo, although variations in gambling severity intergroup measures at the beginning of the trial were complicated interpretations.

7.3 Successful Problem Treatment

Gambling with medications that decrease impulses and increase inhibitions. Researchers found positive results at the annual meeting of the American College of Neuropsychopharmacology (ACNP) in gamblers treated with drugs often used for opioid addictions. Individuals with chronic gambling disorder will continue their gambling activity in the face of their own and their families ' harmful consequences.

Dr. Jon Grant and his University of Minnesota team used cognition-measuring exercises to assess what motivates this intense gambling activity. They included men and women in one of three trials of medicine with a primary diagnosis of pathological gambling. Study sites ranged from 70 participants to 100 participants in number.

Scientists tried to understand how gamblers decide to bet on two brain processes: desire and inhibition.

In order to divide people into groups that reflect discrepancies in their physiology, Grant divided pathological gamblers into two main subtypes: gamblers motivated by compulsion (i.e., individuals who report gambling when temptation becomes too intense to control) and those who do not exhibit normal regulation of impulsive activities (i.e., individuals who report being unable to regulate behavior).

In the first subtype, urge-driven gamblers reacted well to treatment with drugs that block the opioid brain system (e.g., naltrexone) or some neurotransmitter glutamate receptors (e.g., meantime). Grant also found that family history plays a significant role in further refining this group.

Those with a family history of addiction reacted much better to the opioid blocker, which was shown to lessen the temptation to use drugs like alcohol in other studies.

The second subtype, gamblers who have trouble inhibiting their actions and responding to the slightest impulses, respond well to drugs that operate on a particular enzyme, catechol-O-methyl-transferase (COMT), which plays a major role in the prefrontal cortex work. Researchers found that decreasing COMT's function could increase one's ability to inhibit one's willingness to play.

"We can approach the central biology of the disorder with individualized care by recognizing these various subtypes," said Jon Grant, MD, JD, MPH, Associate Professor of Psychiatry at the University of Minnesota and a member of ACNP. "If we look at pathological gambling as an addiction and try to understand the nature of impulses and inhibitions, we can approach drug treatment more effectively," Grant noted that while these findings are promising, and most people are responding to these drugs, there are still some that do not work well.

7.4 Gambling Addiction Treatment Center

Gambling addiction care is not just a matter of replacing the term "gambling" with "alcohol" or "drug" addiction and searching the Internet. Although gambling addiction is a form of impulse-control disorder and the concept of classic addiction definitely applies, the gambling addict requires specialized counseling and therapy to resolve the gambling obsession.

It will not be enough for a treatment center or hospital that is specialized only in drugs and/or alcohol. So, how do you find a treatment center for gambling addiction?

here are a number of gambling addiction treatment centers in the U.S. dedicated exclusively to treating the compulsive gambler. But, they're hard to find.

The good news is that we have clinics and facilities for addiction treatment that also have what is called a gambling line, or a treatment program explicitly designed to address addiction to gambling.

Types of Treatment Programs Residential treatment services offer interdisciplinary care 24 hours a day, seven days a week, both general and advanced. Customers live at the facility and receive services from trained staff to provide specialized treatment for behavioral health problems and other related issues.

These residential treatment facilities can be in freestanding, non-hospital buildings, or in a wing of the hospital. Furthermore, residential treatment services may include homes for treating domestic violence, centers for treating non-hospital addiction, intermediate care facilities, psychiatric centers, and other non-medical arrangements.

Inpatient treatment services offer residential-like but hospital-like care. Inpatient services have as a key component the close collaboration of other service providers and entities, as to Behavioral Health Care Programs, CARF, 2002.

Regular rehabilitation exercises include patients with in-hospital treatment services. The aim of care is to provide a supportive atmosphere that includes medical rehabilitation, support, addiction or mental illness treatment, and supervision.

The National Council on Problem Gambling gives a number of facilities that provide inpatient or residential gambling care. The identified facilities have offered to be included on the web, although there may also be other non-listed qualifying facilities.

The NCPG does not mean inclusion in the collection.

Aid by State the NCPG also has links to a state-by-state map as a starting point for finding help or gathering knowledge on gambling issues. In any search for an approved and accredited gambling addiction treatment center or hospital, it should be used as a starting point.

For example, the California Council on Problem Gambling (CCPG) is a non-profit organization that was founded in 1986 to support problem gamblers and their families by promoting awareness, education, research, prevention, and problem gambling treatment. It's one of the NCPG's 35 local affiliates.

The CCPG site has ties to non-California affiliates, as well as services within the state, including a directory of gambling problem counselors.

Important Factors for Assessing Treatment Center In its approach to gambling addiction treatment, not every treatment facility is the same.

Likewise, for every person seeking help, no one form of treatment works. To be effective, gambling addiction treatment needs to be personally tailored to meet the individual client's needs.

Things to consider including the treatment setting (inpatient, outpatient, individual or group counseling, therapy, 12-stage meetings, etc.), how long the treatment program lasts, philosophical treatment approach, and the specific concerns of the gambling addict and his or her family.

Care Period The duration of care varies with each individual's needs. Clients should discuss their specific needs with the therapist. Some will be handled relatively quickly, while others may take longer, such as learning a new behavior or coping skills to handle the problems of life.

Bottom line is: do not let anything interfere with the search for professional treatment to fix a gambling problem or addiction to gambling. A lot of help is available–if you really want to overcome your gambling compulsion. It will take hard work and dedication, and years of bad behavior will not be easy to undo, but it is possible to do it.

Conclusion

Gambling problems can occur from any part of life to anyone. Your gambling ranges from a fun, harmless diversion to a serious consequence unhealthy obsession. Whether you're betting on football, scratch cards, roulette, poker, or slots — at a casino, track, or online — a gambling problem may strain your relationships, interfere with work and cause a financial catastrophe. You might even do stuff that you never thought you'd do, like running up huge debts or even stealing gambling money.

Gambling addiction is an impulse-control condition, also known as pathological gambling, compulsive gambling or gambling disorder. If you're a compulsive gambler, even if it has negative consequences for you or your loved ones, you can't control the temptation to play. You're going to play whether you're positive or you're negative, broke or clean, and you're going to keep playing irrespective of the consequences— even if you know the odds are against you or you can't afford to lose.

Of course, without being totally out of control, you can also have a gambling problem. Any gambling activity that disrupts your life is a problem gambling. You have a gambling problem if you are obsessed with gambling, wasting more and more time and money on it, chasing losses, or gambling in spite of serious consequences in your life.

The addiction or problem with gambling is often associated with other disorders of behavior or mood. Some gamblers with problems of substance abuse, unmanaged ADHD, stress, depression, anxiety, or bipolar disorder often suffer. You will also need to tackle these and any other underlying causes to solve your gambling issues.

Although stopping gambling can sound like you're helpless, there are plenty of things you can do to solve the issue, restore your relationships and finances, and eventually regain control over your life.

References

- American Psychiatric Association, Diagnostic and Statistical Manual of Mental Disorders, American Psychiatric Association, Washington, DC, USA, 4th edition, 1994.

- G. T. Ladd and N. M. Petry, "Gender differences among pathological gamblers seeking treatment," Experimental and Clinical Psychopharmacology, vol. 10, no. 3, pp. 302–309, 2002. View at Publisher · View at Google Scholar · View at Scopus

- M. N. Potenza, M. A. Steinberg, S. D. McLaughlin, R. Wu, B. J. Rounsaville, and S. S. O'Malley, "Gender-related differences in the characteristics of problem gamblers using a gambling helpline," The American Journal of Psychiatry, vol. 158, no. 9, pp. 1500–1505, 2001. View at Publisher · View at Google Scholar · View at Scopus

- H. J. Shaffer, R. A. LaBrie, D. A. LaPlante, and R. C. Kidman, The Iowa Department of Public Health Gambling Treatment Services: Four Years of

Evidence, Harvard Medical School, Boston Mass, USA, 2002.

- C. Guerreschi, "Le Frontiere del Gioco D'Azzardo," Conferenza sul Gioco D'Azzardo Patologico, Kolpinghaus, 1998.

- G. Serpelloni, "Il Gioco d'Azzardo Patologico in Italia," The Italian Journal on Addiction, vol. 2, pp. 3–4, 2012. View at Google Scholar

- C. Villella, G. Martinotti, M. di Nicola et al., "Behavioural addictions in adolescents and young adults: results from a prevalence study," Journal of Gambling Studies, vol. 27, no. 2, pp. 203–214, 2011. View at Publisher · View at Google Scholar · View at Scopus

- American Psychiatric Association, DSM-5: Development website, 2014, http://www.dsm5.org/Pages/Default.aspx.
  C. Reilly and N. Smith, "The Evolving Definition of

Pathological Gambling in the DSM-5," National Center of Responsible Gaming, 2013.

- F. Angelucci, G. Martinotti, F. Gelfo et al., "Enhanced BDNF serum levels in patients with severe pathological gambling," Addiction Biology, vol. 18, no. 4, pp. 749–751, 2013. View at Publisher · View at Google Scholar · View at Scopus

- M. N. Potenza, "Neurobiology of Gambling Behaviors," Current Opinion in Neurobiology, vol. 23, no. 4, p. 6607, 2013. View at Google Scholar
 M. N. Potenza, "The neurobiology of pathological gambling," Seminars in clinical neuropsychiatry, vol. 6, no. 3, pp. 217–226, 2001. View at Google Scholar · View at Scopus

- S. L. McElroy, J. I. Hudson, K. A. Phillips, P. E. Keck, and H. G. Pope, "Clinical and theoretical implications of a possible link between obsessive-compulsive and impulse control disorders,"

Depression, vol. 1, pp. 121–132, 1993. View at Google Scholar

- C. Blanco, P. Moreyra, E. V. Nunes, J. Sáiz-Ruiz, and A. Ibáñez, "Pathological gambling: addiction or compulsion?" Seminars in Clinical Neuropsychiatry, vol. 6, no. 3, pp. 167–176, 2001. View at Google Scholar · View at Scopus

- N. El-Guebaly, T. Mudry, J. Zohar, H. Tavares, and M. N. Potenza, "Compulsive features in behavioral addictions: the case of pathological gambling," Addiction, vol. 107, no. 10, pp. 1726–1734, 2012. View at Publisher · View at Google Scholar

Printed in Great Britain
by Amazon